The Joy of MUFFINS

The *International* Muffin Cook Book

by

Genevieve Farrow

and

Diane Dreher

GOLDEN WEST ☼ **PUBLISHERS**

Front cover photo by Sollecito Photography, Inc., of Sunnyvale, CA

Cover design by Bruce Fischer/The Art Studio

Library of Congress Cataloging-in-Publication Data

Farrow, Genevieve
  The Joy of Muffins

  Includes index

  1. Muffins 2. Cookery, International I. Dreher, Diane
    II. Title

TX770.M83F37 1989   641.8'15   89-1727

ISBN 0-914846-40-X

Printed in the United States of America

6th printing, ©1994

Information in this book is deemed to be authentic and accurate by authors and publisher. However, they disclaim any liability incurred in connection with the use of information appearing in this book.

Golden West Publishers   (602) 265-4392
4113 N. Longview Ave.
Phoenix, AZ 85014, USA

Golden West Publishers books are available at special discounts to schools, clubs, organizations and businesses for use as fund-raisers, premiums and special promotions.
Send inquiry to Director of Marketing.

Need a fund-raiser?
We can produce a book like this for your organization or club!
For more information contact:
"The Book Studio," c/o Golden West Publishers
4113 N. Longview, Phoenix, AZ 85014, (602) 274-6821

Dedication

We dedicate this book to our husbands
Lyle Farrow and Gwilym Stover,
whose creativity and cooperation
made many of these recipes possible
and also
to the hope of greater creativity,
understanding and peace
throughout the world

Muffin Troubleshooting Guide

Have you ever noticed that when some people make the same recipe they get different results?

Why does this happen? Many things can make a difference. We cannot overemphasize the importance of mixing time. Stirring for 10 seconds produces light, tender muffins. Stirring too long breaks down the gluten and produces tough, hard muffins that could be used as hockey pucks.

Often the ingredients vary. Something as simple as using small, medium or large eggs can alter the ratio of liquid to dry ingredients. Oven temperatures vary—375 degrees in one oven may actually be 350 degrees in another. Experienced cooks learn to make adjustments.

This quick troubleshooting guide will help if you find your muffins less than perfect.

Muffins are hard as baseballs.

- Too much flour—not enough liquid.
  Adjust your ingredients, using one-fourth cup less flour.

- Stirring too long and too hard. Remember: mix only 10 seconds for best results.

Muffins are flat and spreading out all over the top of the muffin tins.

- Muffin pans are too full. Most recipes advise filling pans only two-thirds full.

- Too much liquid in the batter. Adjust your ingredients, using ⅛ to ¼ cup less liquid.

- You forgot to preheat the oven. A slow start can give muffins a "flat top."

Muffins are tough and soggy.

- Overmixing, which toughens the dough. Mix batter only 10 seconds next time.

- Underbaking could also be the problem. Remember: ovens vary greatly in temperature. Try turning your oven up 25 degrees and shortening the baking time.

Muffins rise high and then fall flat in the center.

- Not enough flour. Increase flour about one-fourth cup. Sometimes eggs are so large that they increase the ratio of liquid ingredients.

Muffins do not brown evenly.

- Oven rack too high or too low. Muffins baked on lowest rack may burn on the bottom before they're done on top. Muffins baked on highest rack get too brown on top. Always use middle rack in your oven for even browning.

Contents

Introduction

Our muffin recipes have been internationally inspired. Throughout history, every culture has had its own characteristic form of the staff of life. And nearly every culture has its "quick bread," baked simply, daily, as a ritual of mealtime.

The four corners of the world have all produced similar round, flat breads, formed by hand and baked on a griddle or baking stone. The Middle East has given us flat, hollow "pita" bread, so great for stuffing as sandwiches; India has developed chapati, a perfect complement to curry; France has contributed its marvelous crepes; and Mexico has provided delicious tortillas.

Before the advent of ovens, the Welsh made "pice ar y man," small pancake-like cakes, flavored with cinnamon and nutmeg, and bursting with raisins or currants. Ancestors of modern muffins, these delicious cakes are still served today. Our recipe for Welsh Tea Muffins is adapted from a traditional Welsh cake recipe.

Before quick breads became widespread, bread-making was laborious and slow. In 14th century England, bread was made by casting light wheat flour, called "manchet," salt and warm water together in a wooden tub. This was mixed with ale barm—the foamy yeast that appears on top of malt liquors as they ferment. The dough was stirred or blended with the bare feet, covered with a cloth, left to rise, and finally formed into loaves and baked in a primitive brick oven.

European breads from the Middle Ages through the Renaissance were variations on this formula, adding barley, rye and oats to the list of flours. Bread was often baked communally in large brick ovens "preheated" by building a roaring fire inside to warm the bricks. At home, baking was done either in Dutch ovens on the family hearth, or in rudimentary "pot ovens" set outside over a small fire.

When Europeans came to the New World, they discovered a new ingredient, corn meal. New England colonists learned to make corn pone, hoe cakes and johnny cakes from the Indians. The settlers considered corn bread a kind of health food. They made corn pone by mixing corn meal, water and salt by hand, shaping the dough into small cakes to cook before an open fire. Hoe cakes were simply corn pone cooked on the blade of a hoe in the fields at noon by hungry field workers. Johnny cakes, actually "journey cakes," were small cornmeal cakes carried on a long journey. The many corn muffin recipes in this book reflect America's heritage from the Indian and Hispanic cultures.

Muffins themselves have a varied history. English muffins or crumpets, developed in the early 1700s, are light circular sponge cakes, made from milk, flour, yeast and salt, and originally cooked on a bakestone.

Muffins as we know them appeared after the development of baking powder in the 1840s. Baking powder was originally sold as separate packets of baking soda and cream of tartar. When combined in the muffin batter, a chemical reaction between these acid and alkali ingredients produces bubbles of carbon dioxide, which make the muffins rise. Other acid ingredients such as buttermilk, sour cream and yogurt also combine with soda to produce this chemical reaction.

In 1855, a Boston company combined soda and cream of tartar in a cornstarch base to prevent their interaction until the liquid batter begins the rising process. This is the baking powder we use today.

All quick breads use the acid/alkali rising technique, which is indeed "quick" because the rising process begins while the batter is still in the bowl and is accelerated by the heat of the oven.

A secret in producing perfect muffins is to be "quick" in blending the ingredients. Too much stirring beats the bubbles right out of the batter and produces flat, tough muffins. So, mix quickly and pop the muffins into a pre-heated oven to let the quick-rising process work at its best. Then set your timer and let the fragrance of fresh-baked muffins fill your household and take you on a taste tour of the globe.

Jen Farrow

Marie Dehn

Morning Muffins

Treat yourself to something special in the morning. Bake up a batch of our morning muffins to enjoy all week and start every day with a smile.

Many busy people bake muffins on weekends when they can linger over more luxurious breakfasts, then freeze the remaining muffins in plastic bags. Frozen muffins popped into the microwave for less than one minute on "reheat" taste like they're fresh baked and can be ready long before your coffee is perked. Even with a conventional oven, you can reheat frozen muffins while taking your morning shower.

Apple Muffins

To begin, we offer four marvelous apple muffin recipes—a novel approach to that "apple a day." Since apples are naturally sweet, you can even cut down on the sugar in these recipes and still have delicious muffins.

Dutch Apple Muffins

The Dutch love apples and serve them in a variety of dishes from apple pancakes and apple fritters, to apples cooked with vegetables, and a hearty main course of apples, potatoes and bacon called *hete bliksem*. These muffins were inspired by delicious Dutch apple pie. Try them some morning with yogurt or sharp cheese.

1½ cups chopped
 peeled APPLES
1 cup RAISINS or currants
2 tsp. LEMON JUICE
½ tsp. ground CARDAMON
 or cinnamon
2½ cups all purpose FLOUR

½ cup SUGAR
¼ tsp. SALT
4 tsp. BAKING POWDER
2 large EGGS
1 cup WHIPPING CREAM
¼ cup BUTTER, melted
 or margarine

Mix apples and raisins with lemon juice and spice. Set aside. In a large bowl, stir the dry ingredients together well. In another bowl lightly beat the eggs with the cream and butter. Add to dry ingredients along with the apples. Stir only until dry ingredients are moistened. Spoon into greased muffin tins and bake until golden brown.

Bake at 400 degrees about 18 minutes • Makes 20 muffins.

• All recipes should be baked in two-inch muffin tins.

Danish Applesauce Muffins

Spice up your breakfast with delicious Danish applesauce muffins, based on the *aeblekage* or apple cake popular throughout Denmark.

1 cup unsweetened
  APPLESAUCE
½ cup DARK BROWN SUGAR
  packed
½ cup SHORTENING, melted
1¾ cups unbleached FLOUR

1 tsp. BAKING SODA
½ tsp. SALT
1 tsp. ground CINNAMON
½ tsp. ground CLOVES
½ cup WALNUTS (optional)

Mix applesauce, brown sugar, and shortening together in large bowl. Sift flour, baking soda, salt, cinnamon and cloves in another bowl. Make a well in the center of dry ingredients and add applesauce mixture. Stir together, folding as lightly as possible. Spoon into greased muffin tins and bake until lightly browned. The addition of walnuts to the recipe adds a crunch taste and a delicious flavor, if you wish.

Bake at 375 degrees 25 to 30 minutes • Makes 12 muffins

Brazilian Carioca Spice Muffins

Brazilian carioca lemon spice cake provided the inspiration for these delicate spice muffins, filled with applesauce. Serve them for that special brunch or midmorning coffee break.

1½ cups FLOUR
¼ cup white SUGAR
¼ cup BROWN SUGAR
1½ tsp. BAKING POWDER
½ tsp. SODA
¼ tsp. GINGER
½ tsp. CINNAMON
¾ tsp. MACE

pinch SALT
2/3 cup chopped NUTS
1 Tbsp. grated LEMON RIND
2 EGGS
2 Tbsp. BUTTER, melted
1 cup BUTTERMILK
½ cup APPLESAUCE mixed
  with ¼ tsp. CINNAMON

Mix flour, sugar, brown sugar, baking powder, soda, and spices. Add chopped nuts and grated lemon rind, blending well. In another bowl, whisk eggs, butter, and buttermilk, adding quickly to dry ingredients. Fill muffin cups one-half full. Add one spoonful of applesauce, then cover with batter. Bake until lightly browned.

Bake at 400 degrees 20 minutes • Makes 12 muffins.

Norwegian Apple Muffins

Norwegian *eplepai* or apple pie, the inspiration for these delicious muffins, is baked full of tart apples, cinnamon, and walnuts. We added cranberries, popular throughout Scandinavia, for extra taste appeal.

½ cup BROWN SUGAR
1½ cups WHOLE WHEAT FLOUR
1 cup OATMEAL
1 tsp. CINNAMON
½ tsp. NUTMEG
1 tsp. SODA
1 tsp. BAKING POWDER

1 cup WALNUTS
2 EGGS, beaten
¾ cup APPLESAUCE
1/3 cup BUTTER or margarine, melted
¾ cup canned whole CRANBERRIES

Combine brown sugar, flour, oatmeal, spices, soda, baking powder, and nuts in a large bowl. Mix eggs, applesauce, melted butter, and cranberries together. Pour into center well in dry ingredients and mix quickly. Fill muffin pans three-quarters full and bake until done.

Bake at 375 degrees 20 minutes • Makes 12 muffins.

• Fill muffin cups three-fourths full (unless otherwise indicated).

Oat Bran Muffins

A common expression in the mid-western area is "A horse can work all day on one bucketful of oats." Now people everywhere in the United States are becoming aware of foods necessary for abundant health and energy. This is a recipe filled with energy producing foods.

1 cup OAT BRAN
2/3 cup OATMEAL
1/3 cup wholewheat FLOUR
2/3 cup unbleached FLOUR
1/3 cup RAISINS
1/2 cup WALNUTS, chopped
1 Tbsp. BAKING POWDER

1 tsp. SODA
1 EGG
1 1/2 cups BUTTERMILK
1/4 cup MAPLE SYRUP
6 Tbsp. melted BUTTER
   or margarine

Combine the first eight ingredients in a large bowl and stir until well mixed. In a smaller bowl whisk the egg, buttermilk, maple syrup and melted shortening. Add the moist ingredients to the dry ones in the large bowl, stirring until incorporated well. Spoon into muffin tins which have been sprayed with a non-stick solution and bake until brown.

Bake at 375 degrees 25 minutes • Makes 15 muffins.

Wheat-Free Muffins

Allergic to wheat flour or wheat products? Try these for a change of taste.

1 cup OAT BRAN
1/2 cup CORNMEAL
1 cup RICE FLOUR
1 cup COCONUT
1/2 cup RAISINS
1 Tbsp. BAKING POWDER

1 tsp. SODA
SALT, optional
1 cup BUTTERMILK
2 large EGGS
1/3 cup BROWN SUGAR
1/4 cup SAFFLOWER OIL

Combine the first eight ingredients. Whisk together the buttermilk, eggs, sugar and oil. Pour into the dry ingredients stirring quickly. Spoon into muffin pans.

Bake at 375 degrees 15 minutes • Makes 15 muffins.

Easy Oat Bran Muffins

1 cup OAT BRAN	2 cups BUTTERMILK
1 cup OATMEAL	

Let above mixture stand for one hour to soak up cereals.

2 EGGS	6 Tbsp. melted BUTTER
½ cup BROWN SUGAR	or margarine or oil

Whisk eggs with brown sugar and shortening to melt sugar. Add to oat bran, oatmeal, buttermilk mixture.

1¾ cups FLOUR	1 Tbsp. BAKING POWDER
SALT, if desired	1 tsp. SODA

Then sift flour with baking powder and soda into moist mixture. Combine quickly and spoon into oiled muffin pans and bake.
Bake at 400 degrees 20 minutes • Makes 22 muffins

Double Nut—Double Oat Muffins

The present oat bran rage to reduce cholesterol for heart patients and as a prevention for others, is a valid reason to bake your own muffins. They taste good and are good for you. The nuts provide protein along with the egg.

1 cup OAT BRAN	½ cup chopped ALMONDS
1 cup quick OATMEAL	1 cup plain YOGURT
1 cup unbleached FLOUR	1 cup BUTTERMILK
1 tsp. SODA	1 jumbo EGG
1 Tbsp. BAKING POWDER	1 tsp. VANILLA
½ tsp. SALT	4 Tbsp. melted BUTTER or oil
½ cup chopped PECANS	½ cup dark BROWN SUGAR

Measure the first eight dry ingredients into a large bowl and stir until well blended.

In a smaller bowl whisk together the next six ingredients. Combine quickly and spoon into greased muffin pans and bake on shelf placed in middle of the preheated oven.
Bake at 400 degrees 18 minutes • Makes 18 muffins.

Oat Bran Applesauce Muffins

Combine good taste and nutrition with these delicious muffins.

2 cups OAT BRAN
¼ cup unbleached FLOUR
¼ cup chopped NUTS
¾ cup RAISINS
3 tsp. BAKING POWDER
1 tsp. SODA

1 tsp. CINNAMON (optional)
¼ cup BROWN SUGAR
1 EGG or 2 egg whites
1 cup APPLESAUCE
¾ cup BUTTERMILK
2 Tbsp. VEGETABLE OIL

Combine oat bran, flour, nuts, raisins, baking powder, soda, cinnamon and brown sugar in a large bowl. Mix egg, applesauce, buttermilk and vegetable oil in another bowl. Blend quickly with dry ingredients. Fill greased muffin tins two-thirds full. Test for doneness with toothpick, which should come out moist but not wet.

Bake at 425 for 15-17 minutes • Makes 16 muffins.

Oat Bran Deluxe Muffins

1 cup OAT BRAN
1½ cups BUTTERMILK
1 EGG

½ cup BROWN SUGAR
4 Tbsp. SAFFLOWER OIL

Combine the above and let stand 20 minutes or more to soak up the bran.

1½ cups FLOUR
1 Tbsp. BAKING POWDER
1 tsp. SODA

1½ tsp. CINNAMON
½ cup chopped WALNUTS
½ cup RAISINS

Stir together the above six ingredients. Combine with the buttermilk-bran mixture. Spoon into muffin pans and bake until brown on top.

Bake at 400 degrees 18 to 20 minutes • Makes 16 muffins.

• All muffin cups should be greased or sprayed before filling with batter (unless otherwise indicated).

Kansas Sunflower Oat Bran Muffins

Roasting the sunflower seeds until they are light brown is the secret to these tasty and unusual muffins.

1 cup SUNFLOWER SEEDS

Heat oven to 350 degrees and put sunflower seeds into a pan. Roast until they are brown and well done. Set aside.

½ cup OAT BRAN   **1½ cups BUTTERMILK**
½ cup CORNMEAL

Soak oat bran and cornmeal in buttermilk for one hour.

1 large EGG   **3 Tbsp. melted SHORTENING**
½ cup dark BROWN SUGAR   **or oil**
1 tsp. VANILLA

Whisk together the egg, brown sugar, vanilla and shortening. Stir until the sugar is melted. Add these ingredients to the buttermilk, oat bran, cornmeal mixture above.

1½ cups unbleached FLOUR   **1 tsp. SODA**
1 Tbsp. BAKING POWDER   **½ tsp. SALT (optional)**

Stir flour, baking powder, soda and salt together well. Add the sunflower seeds to this mixture.

Add the dry ingredients (with sunflower seeds) to the buttermilk mixture.

Stir (not over 10 seconds) to blend. Spoon into muffin pans.

Bake at 400 degrees 15 minutes • Makes 16 muffins.

• To store muffins, simply freeze them in tightly-closed plastic bags after letting them cool. Muffins keep in the freezer up to three months. Just thaw them out when ready to use.

Maple Oat Bran Muffins

2 cups BUTTERMILK
2 EGGS or
  3 EGG WHITES
3 Tbsp. SAFFLOWER OIL
½ cup MAPLE SYRUP
3 cups OAT BRAN CEREAL
  any brand

½ cup OAT BRAN
2 cups FLOUR
2 Tbsp. BAKING POWDER
1½ tsp. SODA
½ tsp. SALT
1 cup PECANS, chopped

In a large bowl combine buttermilk, eggs or whites, oil, syrup, oat bran cereal, and oat bran. Stir to blend and allow to stand while you assemble the flour, baking powder, soda, salt and pecans in another bowl. Combine quickly and spoon into muffin tins. Bake on center shelf until brown.

Bake at 375 degrees 20 minutes • Makes 22 muffins.

Oat Bran Spice Muffins

1 cup OAT BRAN
1 cup wholewheat FLOUR
1 cup unbleached FLOUR
1 Tbsp. BAKING POWDER
1½ tsp. BAKING SODA
1 tsp. CINNAMON

1 cup chopped WALNUTS
1 cup unpeeled APPLE, grated
½ cup BROWN SUGAR
1½ cups BUTTERMILK
3 EGG whites
5 Tbsp. SAFFLOWER OIL

Blend the first eight ingredients together well. Dissolve the brown sugar in the buttermilk, add egg whites and oil. Whisk until well mixed. Combine with dry ingredients quickly not stirring over 10 seconds. Spoon into muffin pans and bake.

Bake at 400 degrees 20 minutes • Makes 20 muffins.

Cereal Oat Bran Muffins

2 cups unbleached FLOUR
1 tsp. SALT
2 Tbsp. BAKING POWDER

1½ tsp. SODA
1 tsp. CINNAMON
1 cup PECANS, chopped

Combine the flour, salt, baking powder, soda, cinnamon and pecans in a large bowl. Stir until well mixed.

2 cups BUTTERMILK
1/3 cup SAFFLOWER OIL or
   margarine, melted
3 EGG WHITES

½ cup BROWN SUGAR
2 cups OAT BRAN CEREAL
   any kind
1 cup OAT BRAN

In a smaller bowl combine the buttermilk, oil, egg whites, sugar and whisk until sugar is dissolved. Then add the oat bran cereal and oat bran. Stir until well mixed. Let stand about five minutes so the buttermilk will begin to soak up the cereal and oat bran.

Pour the above mixture into the flour, salt, baking powder, soda, cinnamon and pecan mixture. Blend for 10 seconds until dry ingredients are well blended into the moisture. Spoon into muffin pans which have been sprayed with a non-stick solution.

It is best to always put the nuts into the flour mixture so they will be coated with the dry ingredients. This prevents them from all settling to the bottom of the muffin pans.

Bake at 375 degrees 25 to 28 minutes • Makes 20 muffins.

• Let muffins stand a minute or two before removing from tins. They come out more easily that way. Often, you can simply turn the pan upside down over a board and the muffins fall right out. Sometimes you may have to help them out by running a knife along the side of each muffin cup.

Jamaican Banana Pecan Muffins

Jamaican banana bread, a teatime favorite throughout the Caribbean, is the inspiration for these banana pecan muffins.

1½ cups all-purpose FLOUR
2 tsp. BAKING POWDER
½ tsp. SODA
½ tsp. SALT
½ cup SUGAR
¼ tsp. grated NUTMEG
1 cup unprocessed BRAN

1 cup chopped PECANS
1½ cups mashed BANANAS
2 Tbsp. WATER
1 tsp. VANILLA
1 beaten EGG
¼ cup BUTTER, melted
¾ cup RAISINS (optional)

Mix flour, baking powder, soda, salt, sugar, nutmeg and bran. Stir well. Add pecans. In a small bowl, mix the mashed bananas, water, vanilla, egg and melted butter. Stir well with whisk. Combine quickly with the dry ingredients. Fill greased muffin cups three-fourths full and bake until tester comes out clean.

Bake at 375 degrees 20 to 25 minutes • Makes 18 muffins

Hawaiian Banana Nut Muffins

Hawaiian banana nut muffins are sure to please your palate in the morning or for tea later in the day. Make them with macadamia nuts for true Hawaiian flavor.

2½ cups FLOUR
¾ cup SUGAR
1¼ tsp. BAKING POWDER
1¼ tsp. SODA
1 tsp. SALT
3 EGGS

2/3 cup BUTTER
   or margarine, melted
2/3 cup BUTTERMILK or yogurt
1¼ cups mashed BANANAS
   (3 medium)
2/3 cup chopped MACADAMIA
   NUTS or walnuts

Sift together the flour, sugar, baking powder, soda and salt in a large bowl. In a smaller bowl, beat eggs and blend together with margarine and buttermilk. Add mashed bananas to this mixture. Make a well in the dry ingredients and add the banana-egg-milk mixture, mixing lightly. Fold in the chopped nuts. Spoon into greased muffin cups and bake until golden brown.

Bake at 350 degrees 20 to 25 minutes • Makes 24 muffins.

Blueberry Muffins

Sunday morning in the country with the sun pouring in the windows and blueberry muffins baking in the oven... Recapture this feeling with your own fresh-baked muffins, chock full of Oregon blueberries. If you can save any from the weekend, freeze them in plastic bags for the rest of the week. You might have to double the recipe to have any left.

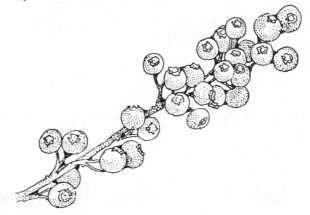

Classic Blueberry Muffins

2 cups FLOUR
¼ cup SUGAR
3 tsp. BAKING POWDER
½ tsp. SALT

2 EGGS
¾ cup MILK
¼ cup melted BUTTER
1 cup washed BLUEBERRIES

Mix together dry ingredients in a large bowl. In another bowl, whisk eggs, milk and melted butter. Make a well in the dry ingredients and pour in liquid ingredients, blending quickly. Fold in blueberries. Spoon batter into greased muffin cups and bake until golden brown.
Bake at 400 degrees 20-30 minutes • Makes 12 muffins.

Blueberry Corn Muffins

1 cup all purpose FLOUR
¾ cup yellow CORNMEAL
¼ cup SUGAR
1½ tsp. BAKING POWDER
½ tsp. SODA
½ tsp. SALT (optional)

1 EGG
½ cup BUTTERMILK
½ cup (1 stick) BUTTER, melted
1½ cups BLUEBERRIES
   (fresh or frozen thawed)

Mix dry ingredients in a large bowl. Beat egg, buttermilk and melted butter in smaller bowl. Add to flour mixture and stir just until flour is moistened. Fold in blueberries. Spoon batter into greased muffin tins and bake until lightly brown. Serve warm.

Bake at 425 degrees 20 to 25 minutes • Makes 12 muffins.

Blueberry Buttermilk Muffins

2½ cups FLOUR
1½ tsp. BAKING POWDER
½ tsp. SODA
¾ cup SUGAR
pinch SALT

2 EGGS, beaten
1 cup BUTTERMILK
1 cube BUTTER (¼ lb.)
1½ cups fresh BLUEBERRIES

Sift dry ingredients together in a large bowl. In another bowl, whisk eggs, buttermilk and butter that has been melted and browned slightly. Make a well in dry ingredients and pour in liquid ingredients, mixing quickly. Fold in blueberries. Spoon batter into greased muffin cups and bake until golden brown.

Bake at 400 degrees 20-30 minutes • Makes 24 muffins.

Bran Muffins

Throughout the golden state from San Francisco to San Diego, Californians enjoy bran muffins for breakfast, tea and coffee breaks. No muffin collection would be complete without a generous sampling of bran muffins, which are not only delicious, but also a digestive aid.

Bran muffins are delicious warm, spread with butter or margarine. But try a nutritious spread of applesauce, ricotta cheese or light cream cheese for a change.

If you're running late some morning, don't skip breakfast. Pop a couple of bran muffins into your briefcase to enjoy on the train or at your desk along with morning coffee. Muffins are the perfect portable breakfast.

Bonnie's Favorite Bran Muffins

Gen's daughter Bonnie contributed this recipe, and recommends adding coconut for a different taste treat.

½ cup (1 stick) BUTTER
  or margarine
¾ cup white SUGAR
½ cup BROWN SUGAR
2 cups BUTTERMILK
2 EGGS

3 cups whole BRAN CEREAL
3 cups all-purpose FLOUR
1 tsp. SALT
2 tsp. BAKING SODA
½ cup chopped NUTS, RAISINS
  or COCONUT (optional)

In a large bowl, cream butter and sugars together. Stir in buttermilk and eggs, then add bran cereal and mix well. Blend together flour, salt and baking soda, then add to other ingredients. Fold in chopped nuts, coconut or raisins as desired. Spoon batter into greased muffin cups and bake. Muffins are delicious served warm with butter or jam.

Bake at 350 degrees 30 minutes • Makes 24 muffins.

Cornmeal-Walnut Bran Muffins

Cornmeal and walnut oil make this a bran muffin with a difference.

1 cup MILK
½ cup BRAN
1 EGG
¼ cup unsalted BUTTER
3 Tbsp. dark BROWN SUGAR
1 cup all-purpose FLOUR

½ cup CORNMEAL
½ cup toasted WALNUTS,
   coarsely-chopped
2 tsp. BAKING POWDER
½ tsp. SALT
1 tsp. WALNUT OIL (optional)

Combine milk and bran in medium bowl and let stand at room temperature overnight or at least eight hours. Stir in egg and melted butter. Fold in dry ingredients which have been well blended, stirring only until dry ingredients are moistened. Grease muffin tins with walnut oil. Spoon batter into muffin tins and bake until brown. Let cool seven minutes before serving.

Bake at 400 degrees 20 to 25 minutes • Makes 12 muffins.

Hollywood Bran Muffins

These muffins are based on a recipe developed years ago by a yoga teacher in Hollywood. Packed full of nutritious natural ingredients, they take a bit longer to put together, but the results are worth it.

2 cups GRAHAM FLOUR
2 cups white FLOUR
1½ cups WHOLE BRAN
½ tsp. SALT
3 tsp. BAKING SODA
½ cup WHEAT GERM
3 Tbsp. BREWER'S YEAST

3 EGGS
1 qt. BUTTERMILK
½ cup HONEY
½ cup BLACK MOLASSES
6 Tbsp. melted BUTTER or
   margarine
1 cup dark RAISINS
1 cup golden RAISINS

Mix dry ingredients together in a very large bowl (this recipe makes lots of muffins!). In a smaller bowl whisk together the eggs, buttermilk, honey, molasses and melted butter. Make a well in the large bowl and blend together wet and dry ingredients, stirring lightly and quickly. Fold in raisins. Spoon into greased muffin tins and bake until muffins test done.

Bake at 300 degrees 40-45 minutes • Makes 36 muffins.

Molasses Bran Muffins

If you like molasses, this recipe will be one of your favorites. It excels in both taste and texture.

½ cup BROWN SUGAR
¼ cup SHORTENING
¼ cup MOLASSES
2 EGGS
1 cup MILK
1½ cups BRAN

1 cup FLOUR
1½ tsp. BAKING SODA
pinch SALT
½ cup RAISINS
½ cup NUTS

Mix first five ingredients with electric mixer. In another bowl mix together bran, flour, soda and salt. Add dry ingredients quickly to liquid mixture. Fold in raisins and nuts. Spoon into muffin tins and bake until muffins test done.

Bake at 400 degree 15 to 20 minutes • Makes 18 muffins.

Honey Nut Bran Muffins

Lyle Farrow developed this recipe after enjoying a similar muffin for breakfast in San Bernardino. The honey and nuts on the bottom add a festive touch to these muffins. Delicious for brunch or tea.

1 cup HONEY
½ cup WATER
½ cup WALNUTS
1 cup whole wheat FLOUR
1 cup BRAN
1 cup BRAN CEREAL

1 tsp. SODA
3 tsp. BAKING POWDER
1 tsp. SALT
2 EGGS
1 cup SOUR CREAM
1 cup RAISINS

Grease muffin tins or use lecithin spray. Mix honey and one-half cup water in a pan and warm on the stove until blended. Spoon one tablespoon walnuts into each of 18 muffin cups. Then cover nuts with one tablespoon honey/water mixture.

Combine flour, bran, cereal, soda, baking powder and salt in mixing bowl. Whisk eggs with sour cream in another bowl. Add raisins. Also add any remaining honey/water mixture to the wet ingredients. Combine with dry ingredients and stir quickly. Spoon into muffin cups and bake until golden.

Bake at 375 degrees 25 minutes • Makes 18 muffins.

Indio Date Bran Muffins

Indio, in Southern California, is surrounded by a vast desert and arid mountain terrain. Early settlers planted hundreds of acres of date palms of all varieties since they had little water for anything else. Now, however, the trees are being replaced by golf courses, condominiums and windmills to obtain power. After a trip to Indio, Lyle Farrow developed these date bran muffins, delicious for brunch or tea.

1 EGG
1⅓ cup MILK
¼ cup melted salt-free BUTTER
1⅓ cup BRAN CEREAL
1½ cup chopped, pitted DATES

1/3 cup PECANS
1¾ cups all-purpose FLOUR
1 Tbsp. BAKING POWDER
1/3 cup SUGAR

Whisk the eggs with the milk and melted butter. Pour over bran cereal and let stand. In another bowl, combine dates, nuts, flour, baking powder and sugar. Add to wet ingredients, stirring together quickly, and spoon into greased muffin tins. The muffins will rise around the edges first as the batter is thin, but as the dates become warm the batter will rise into delicious breakfast or tea-time muffins.

Bake at 375 degrees about 20 minutes • Makes 15 muffins.

Raisin Bran Muffins

This batter may be kept in the refrigerator up to six weeks and baked hot each morning. Or, bake the entire batch of about 30 and freeze them. They warm up wonderfully.

1 cup BRAN
  (cover with 1 cup boiling
water and let stand 20 min.)
½ cup BUTTER or margarine
¾ cup BROWN SUGAR
3 EGGS
2½ cups FLOUR

2½ tsp. BAKING SODA
½ tsp. SALT
2 cups RAISIN BRAN CEREAL
2 cups BUTTERMILK
1 cup RAISINS
1 cup coarsely-chopped
  WALNUTS

Cover bran with one cup boiling water. Set aside for 20 minutes. Mix shortening, sugar, eggs and bran with water in a food processor. Remove to a large bowl and beat in flour, soda, salt, cereal and buttermilk. Fold in raisins and nuts. Spoon into muffin cups and bake until done.

Bake at 375 degrees 20 minutes • Makes 30 muffins.

Yogurt Bran Muffins

Two cups of yogurt give this bran muffin a special touch.

2 cups all-purpose FLOUR
1½ cups natural BRAN
1½ tsp. BAKING SODA
½ tsp. SALT
1 EGG

2 cups plain YOGURT
½ cup OIL
½ cup dark MOLASSES
  or brown sugar
2/3 cup RAISINS

Thoroughly combine dry ingredients in a large mixing bowl. Whisk together egg, yogurt and other ingredients in another bowl. Make a well in the center of dry ingredients and pour in liquid, blending just until moist: do not overmix. Spoon into greased muffin tins and bake until muffins are set.

Bake at 425 degrees 20 to 25 minutes • Makes 24 muffins.

Bran Muffins with Variations

Bran muffins lend themselves to dozens of variations. Try some of these and discover your favorite combination.

1 cup 100% BRAN,
  unprocessed
1 cup boiling WATER
¼ cup MARGARINE
¼ cup (½ stick) unsalted
  BUTTER, room temperature
1 cup SUGAR

2 EGGS
2 cups BUTTERMILK
2 cups ALL BRAN CEREAL
2½ tsp. BAKING SODA
½ tsp. SALT
2½ cups sifted all-purpose
  FLOUR

Combine 100% bran with water in small bowl. Cream shortening and butter with sugar in medium bowl. Add 100% bran and blend well. Gradually beat in remaining ingredients, blending well after each addition. For variations: add chopped nuts, dates or finely-grated orange peel, pecans, coconut or a spoonful of jelly in the center.

Bake at 400 degrees 20 to 25 minutes • Makes 24 muffins.

Main Course Muffins for Breakfast

If you like the smell of bacon cooking or the taste of ham or sausage and eggs in the morning, try our next three recipes.

German Cornmeal Sausage Muffins

In Germany breakfast is usually enhanced with the combination of breads with hidden sausages. Delicious and satisfying to diners who at first wonder why the rolls are so heavy.

1 cup CORNMEAL
1 cup unbleached FLOUR
4 tsp. BAKING POWDER
½ tsp. SALT
¼ tsp. PEPPER
1 Tbsp. SUGAR

1¼ cups MILK
1 EGG
1/3 cup SAFFLOWER OIL
1 GERMAN SAUSAGE,
    cooked and sliced thick

Blend well the first six ingredients in a large bowl. Then whisk the next three ingredients in a small bowl. Combine quickly.

Spoon enough batter into greased muffin pans to fill half full. Then place a slice of the cooked sausage in center and cover with more batter. Bake on middle rack in preheated oven.

Bake at 425 degrees 18 minutes • Makes 15 muffins.

French Dijon Ham Muffins

Combine the flavors of ham and Dijon mustard for a real breakfast surprise. Try these muffins with scrambled eggs.

1²/₃ cups all-purpose FLOUR
1/3 cup CORNMEAL
¼ cup SUGAR
2 tsp. dry MUSTARD
2 tsp. BAKING POWDER
2/3 tsp. SALT
½ tsp. SODA

⅛ tsp. CLOVES
1 cup finely-chopped
   smoked HAM
2 EGGS, room temperature
1 cup BUTTERMILK
1/3 cup VEGETABLE OIL
3 Tbsp. DIJON MUSTARD

Mix together dry ingredients (first eight). Stir in ham. In another bowl, beat together eggs with buttermilk, oil and Dijon mustard. Pour into a well in center of dry ingredients, mixing quickly. Spoon into muffin cups to three-fourths full and bake until brown. Serve warm.

Bake at 375 degrees 20-25 minutes • Makes 12-14 muffins.

Nebraska Corn and Bacon Muffins

From the cornhusker state comes this hearty breakfast muffin, filled with sweet corn and fresh-cooked bacon. Guaranteed to wake anybody up with a smile.

1 cup FLOUR
1/3 cup CORNMEAL
2 Tbsp. SUGAR
2 tsp. BAKING POWDER
½ tsp. SODA
½ tsp. SALT
2 EGGS

2/3 cup SOUR CREAM
7 Tbsp. SAFFLOWER OIL
1 Tbsp. BACON DRIPPINGS
2/3 cup cooked CORN
   (canned is ok)
4 slices BACON, broiled and
   cut into 1-inch pieces

Combine all dry ingredients. Whisk eggs with sour cream, oil and bacon drippings. Add corn and bacon pieces. Stir wet and dry ingredients together quickly and spoon into muffin tins. Bake until tester comes out clean.

Bake at 375 degrees 20 minutes • Makes 12 muffins.

A miscellany of morning muffins...

English Breakfast Muffins

No English breakfast is complete without orange marmalade. These muffins have it inside, as a surprise. Serve with a traditional English breakfast of scrambled eggs, fried tomatoes and mushrooms with a bit of sausage or soy sausage on the side...and, of course, a steaming pot of tea. Or enjoy them on their own, as lighter fare.

¾ cup all-purpose FLOUR
¾ cup whole wheat FLOUR
1/3 cup SUGAR
2 tsp. BAKING POWDER
2 tsp. GINGER
½ tsp. SODA
¼ tsp. SALT

2 EGGS
1/3 cup SOUR CREAM
1/3 cup fresh ORANGE JUICE
7 Tbsp. BUTTER, melted
1 Tbsp. grated ORANGE PEEL
jar of ORANGE MARMALADE

Mix all dry ingredients in large bowl. Whisk eggs, sour cream, orange juice, butter and orange peel in smaller bowl. Add to dry ingredients, stirring quickly. Fill muffin cups three-fourths full. Spoon one teaspoon orange marmalade in center of each muffin. Bake until brown.

Bake at 400 degrees 20 minutes • Makes 16 muffins.

• Muffins are done when they come away from the sides of the pan and when a toothpick or knife inserted into the center comes out dry.

Swedish Christmas Muffins

For Christmas breakfast or afternoon tea, the Swedish serve a special fruit bread, which inspired these festive muffins. They are as welcome at Easter brunch or dinner, if you have the glazed fruit left over from the holidays or can locate some in the spring.

2 cups unbleached FLOUR
½ cup WHEAT GERM
1 tsp. ground CARDAMON
(buy the whole cardamon
and grind it yourself for
a better flavor)
1 tsp. SALT
½ cup SUGAR
4 tsp. BAKING POWDER

1 tsp. SODA
½ cup chopped ALMONDS
½ cup RAISINS
1 cup glazed MIXED FRUIT
2 EGGS
1 cup BUTTERMILK
½ cup melted BUTTER

Combine the first ten ingredients in a large mixing bowl. Whisk eggs, buttermilk and melted butter. Add to dry ingredients, stirring quickly. Spoon into muffin tins and bake in preheated oven until done.

Bake at 375 for 20 to 22 minutes • Makes 18 muffins.

Swedish Breakfast Muffins

Fast, easy and delicious, these muffins are a 150-year-old family recipe from Stockholm.

2 cups FLOUR
4 tsp. BAKING POWDER
4 Tbsp. SUGAR
pinch SALT

1 EGG
1 cup MILK
2 Tbsp. OIL or
butter, melted

Mix these dry ingredients together in a large bowl. Whisk together egg, milk and oil or butter and pour into a well in center of dry ingredients. Mix lightly and quickly together. Spoon into greased muffin cups and bake until done. Serve hot with butter and maple syrup.

Bake at 375 degrees 20 to 25 minutes • Makes 12 muffins.

Scottish Oatmeal Muffins

Oatmeal is a digestive aid and provides essential protein and minerals. Oats have been served in Scotland for centuries in porridge, bannocks, and the Scottish delicacy, haggis. Try these Scottish oatmeal muffins for a delightful difference in the morning.

1 cup OATMEAL
1⅛ cup BUTTERMILK
1 EGG
½ cup BROWN SUGAR
¼ cup melted SHORTENING, cooled

½ cup unbleached FLOUR
½ cup whole wheat PASTRY FLOUR
1½ tsp. BAKING POWDER
½ tsp. SODA
½ tsp. SALT

Soak oatmeal in buttermilk for one hour. Add egg and beat well. Add sugar and mix. Add cooled shortening. Add white and wheat flour sifted with baking powder, soda and salt. Spoon into greased muffin cups and bake until brown.

Bake at 400 degrees 15 to 20 minutes • Makes 12 muffins.

Creole Breakfast Muffins

Deep-fried rice balls or *calas*, a breakfast tradition in New Orleans, inspired these Creole Breakfast Muffins. Try them warm with syrup or jelly along with a steaming cup of *cafe au lait*.

1½ cups FLOUR
¼ cup SUGAR
1½ tsp. BAKING POWDER
½ tsp. SODA
¼ tsp. SALT
1 tsp. CINNAMON
1 tsp. NUTMEG

1 cup cooked white RICE, cooled
1 EGG
2 Tbsp. BUTTER, melted
1⅛ cup BUTTERMILK
CONFECTIONER'S SUGAR

Mix flour, sugar, baking powder, soda, salt and spices. Stir in rice. Whisk egg, butter and buttermilk, and add quickly to dry ingredients. Spoon into greased muffin cups and bake until done. Remove from muffin tins while still warm, sprinkling tops with confectioner's sugar.

Bake at 400 degrees 15-20 minutes • Makes 12 muffins.

Vermont Maple Syrup Muffins

Do you like the taste of maple syrup? Start your day with buttery hot maple syrup muffins and make your breakfast an experience to remember.

2 cups all-purpose FLOUR
4 tsp. BAKING POWDER
½ tsp. SALT
1 large EGG, room temperature

½ cup MILK
½ cup MAPLE SYRUP
½ cup melted BUTTER

Sift flour, baking powder and salt together. In a separate bowl, whisk egg, milk, syrup and butter. Gradually pour this egg mixture into a well in the bowl with the dry ingredients. Stir quickly. Batter will be lumpy. Do not overbeat or muffins will be tough. Spoon into greased muffin cups and bake until brown, about 15 minutes. Serve warm.

Bake at 400 degrees 15 minutes • Makes 12 muffins.

Spanish Cinnamon Muffins

These Spanish cinnamon muffins, adapted from an original Spanish recipe, are delicious hot from the oven. Serve them for breakfast or mid-morning coffee break.

1½ cups FLOUR
1½ tsp. BAKING POWDER
½ tsp. SODA
¼ tsp. SALT
1½ tsp. CINNAMON

½ cup SUGAR
1 EGG
5 Tbsp. BUTTER, melted
1 cup BUTTERMILK

Sift together flour, baking powder, soda, salt, cinnamon and sugar. In another bowl, whisk egg, melted butter and buttermilk. Make a well in dry ingredients and quickly add liquids, blending lightly. Spoon into greased muffin tins and bake until golden.

Bake at 400 degrees 20 minutes • Makes 12 muffins.

Between Meal Muffins

Muffins are a perfect snack—for morning coffee, afternoon tea or with a slice of cheese for a quick energy boost before launching into a new project or setting off for exercise class.

We include both quick snack muffins and the more luxurious high tea muffins for times you choose to linger and enjoy an afternoon treat, a steaming cup of tea, and conversation with friends.

Belgian Spice Muffins

Based on *pain d'épice*, a spiced bread popular in Belgium. We added a cupful of grated carrots for extra nutrition and taste appeal.

1 cup MILK
1 EGG
3 Tbsp. BUTTER, melted
1 cup BRAN
1 cup all-purpose FLOUR
¼ cup firmly-packed
   BROWN SUGAR
2 tsp. BAKING POWDER
½ tsp. BAKING SODA

½ tsp. SALT
½ tsp. NUTMEG
½ tsp. CINNAMON
1 tsp. grated ORANGE or
   LEMON PEEL (optional)
1 cup grated CARROTS
½ cup RAISINS
½ cup WALNUTS

Blend milk, egg and melted butter in a small bowl. Combine and sift all dry ingredients into a larger bowl. Stir milk mixture into a well in the center of the dry ingredients. Quickly stir in carrots, raisins and walnuts. Spoon into muffin tins to three-fourths full. Bake until golden brown.

Bake at 375 degrees about 15 minutes • Makes 12 muffins.

German Tea Muffins

These muffins are adapted from a recipe for *altdeutsche brotchen*, literally "Old German muffins." Spiced with orange, cinnamon, rum and raisins, they are a delicious accompaniment with coffee or tea.

2 cups all-purpose FLOUR
½ cup SUGAR
½ tsp. CINNAMON
2 tsp. BAKING POWDER
1 Tbsp. grated ORANGE RIND
½ cup chopped ALMONDS
½ cup golden RAISINS

2 EGGS, beaten
¾ cup MILK
½ cup BUTTER, melted
1 tsp. VANILLA
1 Tbsp. RUM or
   ½ tsp. rum flavoring

Mix together flour, sugar, cinnamon, baking powder, grated orange rind, almonds and raisins. In another bowl, beat together eggs, milk, melted butter, vanilla and rum. Make a well in the dry ingredients and add the milk and egg mixture, stirring lightly and quickly. Spoon into greased muffin cups and bake until tester comes out clean and muffins are lightly brown.

Bake at 375 degrees 25-30 minutes • Makes 18 muffins.

Canadian Scone Muffins

Add a special flair to teatime with these Canadian scone muffins, inspired by the scones served for high tea at the Empress Hotel, Victoria, British Columbia. For your own high tea, serve these currant-studded muffins with the traditional butter and jam.

2 cups all-purpose FLOUR	pinch SALT
1 tsp. BAKING POWDER	1 stick (½ cup) BUTTER
½ tsp. SODA	2/3 cup CURRANTS
1 Tbsp. SUGAR	1 to 1¼ cup BUTTERMILK
¼ tsp. CINNAMON	beaten EGG for glaze
⅛ tsp. NUTMEG	

Mix together flour, baking powder, soda, sugar and spices. Cut butter into flour until it resembles coarse meal. Mix in currants. Gradually add buttermilk, until dough is just moist. Batter will be dough-like in consistency. Spoon into greased muffin cups and brush tops with beaten egg to glaze. Bake until done and serve warm.

Bake at 375 degrees 20-25 minutes • Makes 12 muffins.

Irish Jam Muffins

Filled with sparkling berry jam and topped with powdered sugar, these Irish jam muffins are a special treat for tea or dessert.

1½ cups FLOUR	4 Tbsp. BUTTER, melted
1½ tsp. BAKING POWDER	1 cup BUTTERMILK
½ tsp. SODA	½ tsp. LEMON EXTRACT
½ cup SUGAR	1 cup RASPBERRY or
1 tsp. grated LEMON RIND	BLUEBERRY JAM
1 EGG	CONFECTIONER'S SUGAR

Mix together flour, baking powder, soda, sugar and grated lemon rind in a large bowl. Whisk egg with melted butter, buttermilk and lemon extract. Make a well in dry ingredients and quickly add liquid ingredients. Fill greased muffin tins one-half full. Add two spoons of jam and cover with batter. Bake until done, remove from tins after five minutes and sprinkle tops with confectioner's sugar.

Bake at 400 degrees 15-20 minutes • Makes 12 muffins.

Spanish Sherry Nut Muffins

Sherry, which originated in Andalusia, Spain, combines with brown sugar, coffee, dates and nuts in this moist, delicious tea muffin.

1 cup chopped DATES
1/3 cup boiling strong COFFEE
1/3 cup cooking SHERRY
4 Tbsp. BUTTER or margarine
1 tsp. VANILLA
½ tsp. SALT

2 EGGS
2/3 cup dark BROWN SUGAR
2 cups unbleached FLOUR
½ cup BRAN CEREAL
2 tsp. SODA
½ cup chopped PECANS

Cut up dates and put into a large mixing bowl. Pour boiling strong coffee over them and stir well. Then pour in the sherry and add butter. Let stand until butter is soft and melting. (Prepare muffin pans. Preheat oven while this mixture soaks up the date flavor and softens the dates.) Add vanilla, salt, eggs and brown sugar. Stir until sugar is melted and eggs whisked. Brown sugar often becomes hard and lumpy, and it is better to dissolve it beforehand than to have lumps in your muffins.

In a separate bowl mix the flour, bran, soda and pecans. Blend well. Add dry ingredients to the sherry mixture, stirring not over 10 seconds. Spoon into greased muffin pans and bake until brown.

Bake at 375 degrees 18 to 20 minutes • Makes 12 muffins.

Delhi Carrot Muffins

Delhi carrot muffins are inspired by *gajjar halwa*, a grated carrot pudding very popular in northern India. Try them with tea for a real taste treat.

1½ cups SUGAR
1 cup SAFFLOWER OIL
4 EGGS, lightly-beaten
3 cups all-purpose FLOUR
2 tsp. BAKING POWDER

1 tsp. BAKING SODA
½ tsp. SALT
2 cups grated CARROTS
1 cup PISTACHIO NUTS
1 cup WALNUTS

Beat sugar, oil and eggs in medium bowl. Sift dry ingredients together. Gradually stir dry ingredients into oil, egg and sugar mixture. Fold in carrots and nuts. Spoon into greased muffin cups and bake until done. (They begin to brown very quickly.) They are delicious warm.

Bake at 400 degrees 18 to 20 minutes • Makes 24 muffins.

Russian Walnut Muffins

Russian walnut cake, *orechovii tort*, provides the inspiration for Russian walnut muffins. They're wonderful with tea or serve with fresh fruit for a light dessert.

1½ cups all-purpose FLOUR
1 Tbsp. BAKING POWDER
¼ cup BROWN SUGAR
¼ cup white SUGAR
1 cup chopped WALNUTS

1 EGG
1 tsp. VANILLA
⅞ cup MILK
¼ cup BUTTER, melted

Mix flour, baking powder, sugar and brown sugar in a large bowl. Add chopped walnuts. Whisk egg together with vanilla, milk and melted butter. Make a well in the dry ingredients and add the wet ingredients, stirring quickly. Batter will be lumpy. Spoon into greased muffin cups and bake until lightly brown and muffins pull away from sides of tin.

Bake at 375 degrees 20-25 minutes • Makes 12 muffins.

California Gold Muffins

From California's fertile central valley come the apricots and golden raisins that make these muffins a special treat for tea. Try them with iced orange or peppermint herb tea for a sunny day snack.

1½ cups all-purpose FLOUR
½ cup SUGAR
1 tsp. ground CORIANDER
1 tsp. BAKING POWDER
½ tsp. SODA
½ tsp. SALT
¼ tsp. ALLSPICE
2/3 cup grated
    YELLOW SQUASH

1/3 cup finely-chopped
    dried APRICOT
1/3 cup golden RAISINS
2/3 cup finely-grated
    CARROT
2 EGGS
½ cup BUTTER,
    melted and cooled
½ tsp. VANILLA

Mix first seven ingredients in large bowl. Stir in squash, apricots, raisins and carrots. Whisk eggs, butter and vanilla together and add to the dry ingredients. Batter will be lumpy—do not overbeat! Fill greased muffin cups three-fourths full and bake.

Bake at 375 degrees 25 minutes • Makes 12 muffins.

High Sierra Muffins

Campers and hikers in America's High Sierra enjoy a quick energy boost from trail mix, a combination of dried fruits and nuts. These High Sierra Muffins are chock full of fruit, nuts, bran and soy flour for a nutritious, high protein treat.

1¼ cups all-purpose FLOUR
5 Tbsp. SOY FLOUR
1 cup BRAN
¼ cup SUGAR
1 tsp. BAKING POWDER

½ tsp. SODA
1 cup TRAIL MIX
1 EGG
1 cup BUTTERMILK
¼ cup VEGETABLE OIL

Mix flour, soy flour, bran, sugar, baking powder and soda. Add trail mix. In another bowl, whisk egg, buttermilk and vegetable oil. Quickly add to dry ingredients, stirring only ten seconds. Spoon into greased muffin cups and bake until done.

Bake at 400 degrees 20-25 minutes • Makes 12 muffins.

Middle East Orange Date Muffins

The Middle East, a region of many cultures and contrasts, desert date palms and juicy Haifa oranges, provides the key ingredients for these delicious muffins.

1½ to 2 cups chopped DATES
2 large ORANGES
WATER
2 Tbsp. BUTTER, melted
1 tsp. VANILLA
1 EGG
2 cups FLOUR

¼ tsp. SALT
2 tsp. BAKING POWDER
½ tsp. BAKING SODA
2/3 cup white SUGAR
1 cup chopped NUTS
    walnuts and pecans

Chop dates and put into a large mixing bowl. Squeeze juice from two large oranges and add water to fill to one cup. Put orange juice, water and the rind of one orange into the blender and puree. Pour over dates. Let stand about 15 minutes. Add the rest of the ingredients, stir and fill muffin tins to three-fourths full. Bake until brown or until testing knife or toothpick comes out clean.

Bake at 375 degrees about 25 minutes • Makes 17 muffins.

• If you are cholesterol-conscious, you may want to substitute the whites of two (2) eggs for every whole egg in the recipe, since egg whites contain no cholesterol.

Brazilian Orange Muffins

Inspired by *bolo de l'aranja*, delicious Brazilian orange cake, Brazilian orange muffins are wonderful with tea. We added pecans for extra appeal.

Topping:

¼ cup SUGAR	½ tsp. NUTMEG
3 Tbsp. FLOUR	2 Tbsp. BUTTER
½ tsp. CINNAMON	

Mix first four ingredients; cut in butter and set aside.

2 cups all-purpose FLOUR	½ cup ORANGE JUICE
¼ cup SUGAR	½ cup ORANGE MARMALADE
3 tsp. BAKING POWDER	¼ cup SHORTENING, melted
1 tsp. SALT	½ cup PECANS, chopped
1 EGG, beaten	

Mix dry ingredients in a large bowl. In a small bowl blend the egg with the orange juice, marmalade, and melted shortening. Mix together wet and dry ingredients just until blended. Fold in pecans. Spoon into greased muffin cups, sprinkle on topping, and bake until brown.

Bake at 375 degrees 20 to 25 minutes • Makes 12 muffins.

Indian Three-Nut Muffins

These muffins are inspired by *burfi magaz*, a three-nut sweet served for tea time or dessert throughout India. The Indians use pistachio nuts, almonds and melon seeds. We have substituted sunflower seeds for the melon seeds.

1 EGG	¼ cup PISTACHIO NUTS
½ cup MILK	lightly toasted
¼ cup MARGARINE, melted	2 Tbsp. chopped ALMONDS
(½ stick)	or walnuts, lightly toasted
1½ cups all-purpose FLOUR	3 Tbsp. SUNFLOWER SEEDS
½ cup SUGAR	1 Tbsp. BAKING POWDER

Beat egg together with milk and margarine. Stir in remaining ingredients. Spoon into greased muffin cups and bake until golden brown. These flavorful muffins are delicious for tea or dessert.

Bake at 375 degrees 20 to 25 minutes • Makes 10 muffins.

Indonesian Peanut Butter Muffins

Indonesian cuisine makes liberal use of peanuts—as a salad dressing and as *gado-gado*, a sauce served with vegetables at the traditional Rice Table, a meal consisting of rice and up to 22 exotic and spicy side dishes. Try Indonesian peanut butter muffins for tea or snacks. They are filled with protein and children love them.

1¾ cups FLOUR
½ tsp. SALT
3 tsp. BAKING POWDER
1/3 cup SUGAR

¾ cup MILK
1 EGG
1/3 cup SHORTENING
PEANUT BUTTER

Sift together dry ingredients in large bowl. Mix milk, egg and shortening, and add all at once to dry ingredients. Mix only until moist. Batter will be lumpy. Fill greased muffin cups two-thirds full. Drop one teaspoon peanut butter in center of each muffin. Cover with batter. Bake until brown.

Bake at 400 degrees 18 minutes • Makes 12 muffins.

Colonial American Pumpkin Muffins

Pumpkins have become popular in many parts of the world. The Russians enjoy pumpkin pudding, or *Tikvenaia Kasha*, made of pumpkin, eggs, sugar and milk. The inspiration for these muffins comes from Colonial American pumpkin pie, enjoyed by Americans each year with their Thanksgiving and Christmas dinners. But you don't need to wait for the holidays to enjoy these spicy muffins.

1 cup CAKE FLOUR
1 cup all-purpose FLOUR
1 Tbsp. BAKING POWDER
½ tsp. SALT
1 tsp. CINNAMON
½ tsp. NUTMEG

¼ tsp. CLOVES
½ cup BROWN SUGAR
1 EGG, beaten
3 Tbsp. OIL
½ cup PUMPKIN
¾ cup MILK

Sift together first eight ingredients. Whisk egg with oil, pumpkin and milk. Quickly blend wet and dry ingredients. Drop batter into greased muffin pans and bake until done.

Bake at 400 degrees 20 minutes • Makes 12 muffins.

Danish Rum-Raisin Muffins

Rum-flavored desserts became popular in Denmark because of the Danish colonies in the West Indies. Danish rum-raisin muffins are inspired by *romfromage* and *rombudding*, rum cream and rum pudding. They are delicious for tea. Serve them with raspberry jam or whipped cream for real Danish appeal.

Soak overnight:
  1 cup RAISINS
  ½ cup DARK RUM

2 cups all-purpose FLOUR
½ cup SUGAR
1½ tsp. BAKING POWDER

½ tsp. BAKING SODA
¼ tsp. SALT
¼ tsp. NUTMEG
6 Tbsp. BUTTER (¾ stick)
1 cup SOUR CREAM
1 EGG
¾ tsp. VANILLA

Drain raisins, reserving rum. Mix dry ingredients in large bowl. Cut in butter until coarse meal forms. Mix in raisins. Whisk sour cream, egg, vanilla and two tablespoons rum until smooth. Make a well in center of dry ingredients and pour in cream and egg mixture. Fill muffin pans three-fourths full and bake until brown.

Bake at 375 degrees 20 minutes • Makes 18 muffins.

Hungarian Hussar's Muffins

Hungarian Hussar's kisses with their delicate lemon flavor and apricot filling inspired these delicious tea muffins.

1½ cups FLOUR
½ cup SUGAR
½ tsp. grated LEMON RIND
1½ tsp. BAKING POWDER
½ tsp. SODA
½ tsp. SALT

1 large EGG, beaten
4 Tbsp. BUTTER, melted
1 cup BUTTERMILK
2 tsp. LEMON JUICE
APRICOT JAM
¼ cup chopped ALMONDS

Mix flour, sugar, lemon rind, baking powder, soda and salt in large bowl. In small bowl whisk egg, melted butter, buttermilk and lemon juice. Make a well in dry ingredients and quickly add liquid ingredients. Fill greased muffin tins one-half full, then add one spoonful of apricot jam and cover with batter. Sprinkle tops with chopped almonds and bake until golden.

Bake at 400 degrees 15-20 minutes • Makes 12 muffins.

Mexican Flan Muffins

Inspired by Norma MacCaskey's delicious Mexican *flan*, these caramel-kissed muffins are great with tea or after an authentic Mexican meal. Olé!

½ cup SUGAR
1¼ cups boiling WATER
2 cups unbleached FLOUR
3 tsp. BAKING POWDER
½ cup SUGAR

2 EGGS, beaten
1 cup EVAPORATED MILK
2 tsp. VANILLA EXTRACT
3 Tbsp. BUTTER, melted

Grease muffin tins. Caramelize one-half cup sugar by cooking in large saucepan until melted and golden brown, stirring as needed. Slowly and carefully add 1¼ cups boiling water and stir until blended. Pour one tablespoonful into greased muffin tins. Set aside.

Mix together flour, baking powder and sugar. Whisk eggs, evaporated milk, vanilla and melted butter together. Blend with dry ingredients, mixing lightly. Spoon batter into muffin tins and bake until done. After muffins cool for two minutes, gently remove from pans and place upside down on serving tray.

Bake at 375 degrees 20 to 22 minutes • Makes 14 muffins.

Syrian Sesame Muffins

Syrian Sesame Muffins are adapted from the sesame biscuits served throughout the Middle East. Try them warm with butter and honey for tea or with cheese or peanut butter for a light, nutritious snack.

1½ cups unbleached FLOUR
1½ tsp. BAKING POWDER
½ tsp. SODA
¼ tsp. SALT
1/3 cup white SUGAR
1/3 cup BROWN SUGAR

1/3 cup roasted
   SESAME SEEDS
1 EGG
1¼ cups BUTTERMILK
4 Tbsp. BUTTER or
   margarine, melted
1 Tbsp. SESAME OIL

Mix flour, baking powder, soda, salt, white and brown sugar, and sesame seeds in a large bowl. Whisk egg with buttermilk, melted butter and sesame oil. Make a well in dry ingredients and add liquid ingredients quickly. Spoon batter into muffin tins and sprinkle tops with sesame seeds. Bake until golden brown.

Bake at 400 degrees 15-20 minutes • Makes 12-14 muffins.

Portuguese Spice Muffins

For a special treat at tea time, try these spicy Portuguese muffins, flavored with ginger and molasses. They are adapted from an old recipe for Portuguese molasses cookies and are absolutely delicious.

1½ cups FLOUR
½ cup SUGAR
¼ tsp. SALT
½ tsp. CINNAMON
½ tsp. ALLSPICE
¼ tsp. NUTMEG
½ tsp. GINGER

1½ tsp. BAKING POWDER
½ tsp. SODA
1 EGG, beaten
¼ cup MARGARINE, melted
1/3 cup MOLASSES
¾ cup BUTTERMILK

Mix together flour, sugar, spices, baking powder and soda. In another bowl, whisk egg with melted margarine, molasses and buttermilk. Make a well in the dry ingredients and add liquid, stirring lightly. Spoon into greased muffin cups and bake until done.

Bake at 400 degrees 15 to 20 minutes • Makes 12 muffins.

Hawaiian Brown Rice Muffins

A tasty, nutritious combination of brown rice, coconut and pineapple chunks, these Hawaiian brown rice muffins are great for tea or a light afternoon snack.

1 cup unbleached FLOUR
½ cup whole wheat FLOUR
1 tsp. CINNAMON
1 Tbsp. BAKING POWDER
pinch of SALT
½ cup COCONUT

½ cup BROWN RICE, cooked
2 EGGS
2/3 cup MILK
¼ cup SAFFLOWER OIL
1/3 cup BROWN SUGAR
3 slices canned PINEAPPLE

Mix white and whole wheat flour, baking powder, cinnamon, salt, coconut and rice in a large bowl. Whisk eggs, milk, oil and brown sugar in small bowl. Make a well in dry ingredients and quickly stir in the moist ingredients. Spoon into muffin tins and then poke one-eighth piece of pineapple slice into center of each. Bake until golden.

Bake at 375 degrees 25 minutes • Makes 12 muffins.

Czechoslovakian Kolacky Muffins

Czechoslovakian *kolacky*, pastry filled with prunes or dates, inspired these unusual tea muffins.

Filling:

½ cup pitted PRUNES	½ tsp. CINNAMON
1 Tbsp. BUTTER, melted	¼ cup chopped WALNUTS
1 Tbsp. SUGAR	

Place pitted prunes in small bowl and cover with water. Soak overnight or stew in microwave. Drain. Chop finely. Add melted butter, sugar, cinnamon and nuts. Set aside.

1½ cups FLOUR	1 EGG
1/3 cup SUGAR	2 Tbsp. BUTTER, melted
1½ tsp. BAKING POWDER	1 cup BUTTERMILK
½ tsp. SODA	CINNAMON SUGAR
¼ tsp. MACE or allspice	

Combine flour, sugar, baking powder, soda and spice. In another bowl, whisk egg, melted butter and buttermilk. Quickly combine with dry ingredients. Spoon batter into muffin cups one-third full. Add one tablespoon prune filling. Cover with batter until two-thirds full. Sprinkle cinnamon sugar on top and bake until lightly browned.

Bake at 400 degrees 15-20 minutes • Makes 12 muffins.

• Muffins bake best in the middle shelf of your oven. On the lowest shelf, the bottoms brown too quickly. On the highest shelf, the tops brown too soon.

German Streusel Muffins

Hot from the oven and crowned with a delicious streusel topping, German Streusel Muffins are a special treat for afternoon tea.

1/3 cup SHORTENING	1½ tsp. BAKING POWDER
½ cup SUGAR	½ tsp. SALT
1 EGG	¼ tsp. NUTMEG
1½ cups all-purpose FLOUR	½ cup MILK

Mix thoroughly, shortening, sugar and egg. Stir in dry ingredients alternately with milk. Fill muffin pans two-thirds full and bake until done.

Topping:

½ cup SUGAR	1 tsp. CINNAMON
¼ cup ground ALMONDS	½ cup BUTTER

Mix one-half cup sugar, the ground almonds and the cinnamon together well. Melt one-half cup butter. Immediately after baking, roll in melted butter, then in the almond, cinnamon-sugar mixture. Serve hot.

Bake at 350 degrees 20 to 25 minutes • Makes 15 muffins.

Danish Sour Cream Muffins

A land of rich dairy farms, Denmark produces a great abundance of cream each year. The Danes make some of the richest ice cream in the world and have incorporated sour cream into many of their recipes. Serve these delicious, light muffins with strawberry jam for a real Danish flavor.

2 cups all-purpose FLOUR	1 cup PECANS,
2 tsp. BAKING POWDER	chopped coarsely
½ tsp. SALT	2 cups SOUR CREAM
3 heaping Tbsp. SUGAR	2 beaten EGGS
1 tsp. BAKING SODA	

Sift together flour, baking powder, salt, sugar and soda. Stir in chopped pecans. Make a well and pour in the sour cream and beaten egg. Mix only until moistened. Spoon into greased muffin pans and bake until brown.

Bake at 400 degrees 20 to 25 minutes • Makes 12-14 muffins.

Russian Poppyseed Muffins

Russian Poppyseed Muffins were inspired by the honey and poppyseed loaves baked for feast days in Russian monasteries as far back as the 14th century. Try them along with Russian tea—tea sweetened with berry jam.

1¾ cups all-purpose FLOUR
½ tsp. SALT
1½ tsp. BAKING POWDER
½ tsp. BAKING SODA
2 EGGS, beaten
½ cup MILK

1 cup SOUR CREAM
¼ cup OIL
2 tsp. VANILLA (or orange flavoring if you prefer)
1/3 cup HONEY
¼ cup POPPYSEED

Mix the dry ingredients in a large bowl. Beat eggs and add milk, sour cream, oil, vanilla and honey. Make a well in the dry ingredients and add the wet ingredients, stirring lightly for about ten seconds. Fold in poppyseeds. Spoon into greased muffin tins and bake until tester comes out clean.

Bake at 375 degrees 20-25 minutes • Makes 15 muffins.

Indian Curry Muffins

Dried apples, raisins, nuts, coconut and curry powder make these Indian Curry Muffins a delightful treat for midmorning coffee or afternoon tea.

1 cup all-purpose FLOUR
½ cup whole wheat FLOUR
½ cup SUGAR
1½ tsp. BAKING POWDER
½ tsp. SODA
pinch SALT
¾ tsp. CURRY POWDER

1/3 cup RAISINS
2/3 cup dried APPLES, diced
1/3 cup chopped NUTS
2/3 cup shredded COCONUT
1 EGG
1¼ cups BUTTERMILK
3 Tbsp. BUTTER, melted

Mix flour, whole wheat flour, sugar, baking powder, soda, salt and curry powder. Blend in raisins, apples, nuts and coconut. In another bowl, whisk egg, buttermilk and melted butter. Add quickly to dry ingredients. Spoon batter into greased muffin cups and bake until lightly brown.

Bake at 400 degrees 15-20 minutes • Makes 14-16 muffins.

New Orleans Praline Muffins

This muffin was inspired by those irresistible New Orleans pecan pralines—definitely something special at tea time.

1½ cups coarsely-chopped PECANS, toasted

Toast 1½ cups chopped pecans in 300 degree oven for about 20 minutes.

Topping:
    3 Tbsp. BROWN SUGAR   ½ cup toasted PECANS
    1 Tbsp. dairy SOUR CREAM

For topping, mix brown sugar and sour cream together in small bowl. Add one-half cup chopped pecans. Set aside.

1½ cups all-purpose FLOUR	½ cup BUTTER, melted
2 tsp. BAKING POWDER	½ to 2/3 cup MILK
pinch of SALT and ALLSPICE	½ cup MAPLE SYRUP
1 cup toasted PECANS	1 EGG
½ cup BROWN SUGAR	1 tsp. VANILLA

Mix flour, baking powder, salt and spice. Stir in toasted pecans. Whisk sugar, melted butter, milk, syrup, egg and vanilla in medium bowl. Make a well in center of dry ingredients. Add butter mixture and stir only until blended. Fill greased muffin cups three-fourths full. Garnish top of each muffin with one teaspoon of topping mixture. Bake until tester comes out clean. Serve warm.

Bake at 375 degrees 20 minutes • Makes 12-14 muffins.

• Pop frozen muffins into the microwave for one minute or less on "reheat." For conventional ovens, wrap frozen muffins in aluminum foil and heat for 10-15 minutes at 350 degrees.

Swedish Strawberry Muffins

Strawberries grow wild in the fields of Skone in southern Sweden. They are a springtime favorite, signaling the end of the long winter, and Scandinavian strawberry preserves are perhaps the finest in the world. Enjoy these delicious strawberry muffins for tea or dessert.

1¼ cups unbleached FLOUR
2/3 cup OAT BRAN
1½ tsp. BAKING POWDER
½ tsp. SODA
½ cup SUGAR
2 EGGS

4 Tbsp. BUTTER, melted
1 cup BUTTERMILK
½ cup Scandinavian
    STRAWBERRY PRESERVES
¼ cup sliced ALMONDS

Mix together flour, oat bran, baking powder, soda and sugar in a large bowl. In another bowl, whisk eggs with melted butter and buttermilk. Make a well in the dry ingredients and quickly add egg mixture. Fill greased muffin tins one-half full. Add a heaping tablespoon of strawberry preserves, then cover with batter. Top with sliced almonds. Bake until golden brown and tester comes out clean.

Bake at 400 degrees 15-20 minutes • Makes 15 muffins.

Iowa Crunch Muffins

If you like the taste of peanut butter, you'll enjoy these Iowa Crunch Muffins, a family recipe from Eunice Kehoe of Waterloo, Iowa. Try them for a tasty afternoon snack.

Topping:
3 Tbsp. PEANUT BUTTER
4 Tbsp. SUGAR

2 Tbsp. FLOUR
⅛ tsp. SALT

Combine topping ingredients with fork and set aside.

2 cups sifted FLOUR
1 Tbsp. BAKING POWDER
½ tsp. SALT
2 Tbsp. SUGAR

1 EGG, beaten
1 cup MILK
1/3 cup BUTTER or
    margarine, melted

Mix together flour, baking powder, salt and sugar in a large bowl. In another bowl, whisk egg, milk and melted butter. Pour into a well in dry ingredients, mixing lightly and quickly. Fill greased muffin tins two-thirds full and sprinkle on topping.

Bake at 400 degrees 20 minutes • Makes 12 muffins

Caribbean Fruit Muffins

Banana and coconut breads are teatime favorites throughout the Caribbean Islands. Treat yourself to these exotic Caribbean Fruit Muffins. Serve them with iced tea and lime for an authentic Caribbean taste.

2¼ cups OAT or WHEAT BRAN from health food store
2/3 cup unbleached FLOUR
2/3 cup whole wheat FLOUR
1 tsp. BAKING POWDER
2½ tsp. BAKING SODA
¼ tsp. SALT

1½ cups GOLDEN RAISINS
1¼ cups shredded COCONUT
2 EGGS
1 cup BUTTERMILK
½ cup VEGETABLE OIL
1 cup mashed BANANAS
½ cup HONEY

In large bowl, combine bran, flour, whole wheat flour, baking powder, soda, salt, raisins and coconut. Stir until blended. In another bowl, whisk eggs with remaining ingredients. Stir quickly into dry ingredients, mixing just until blended. Spoon equally into greased muffin cups and bake until lightly browned.

Bake at 375 degrees 20 to 25 minutes • Makes 18-24 muffins.

Welsh Tea Muffins

Inspired by the Welsh cake recipe of Mrs. Nan Edwards of Ystradgynlais, Wales, these muffins will fill your kitchen with the aroma of cinnamon, nutmeg and raisins—and disappear quickly once they are served.

1½ cups all-purpose FLOUR
½ cup SUGAR
¼ tsp. SALT
2 tsp. BAKING POWDER
1 tsp. SODA
1 tsp. CINNAMON

½ tsp. NUTMEG
1¼ cups RAISINS
2 EGGS, beaten
1 cup BUTTERMILK
2 Tbsp. MARGARINE, melted

Mix flour, sugar, salt, baking powder, soda, cinnamon and nutmeg in a large bowl. Mix in raisins. Whisk eggs, milk and melted shortening. Make a well in the dry ingredients and add the egg mixture. Stir together quickly. Batter will be lumpy. Fill greased muffin cups two-thirds full and bake until tester comes out clean.

Bake at 400 degrees 20-25 minutes • Makes 12-14 muffins.

Italian Zucchini Muffins

The Italian squash or zucchini turns up in many Italian recipes from main courses such as pasta primavera and zucchini parmesan to delicious side dishes. The inspiration for Italian Zucchini Muffins came from a fragrant zucchini bread baked by an Italian family in Boston.

3 cups all-purpose FLOUR
1 tsp. BAKING POWDER
1 tsp. BAKING SODA
½ tsp. SALT
1 tsp. CINNAMON
1 cup SUGAR
4 EGGS, room temperature

1 cup OIL
2 cups grated ZUCCHINI, unpeeled
1 tsp. VANILLA
1 cup chopped WALNUTS
½ cup GOLDEN RAISINS

Sift flour, baking powder, soda, salt and cinnamon. Set aside.

Combine sugar and eggs in a large bowl and beat at medium speed for two minutes. Gradually add oil in a slow, steady stream, beating constantly for two or three minutes—important. Add zucchini and vanilla, blending well. Stir in walnuts and raisins. Fold in sifted ingredients just until batter is evenly moistened. Do not overmix. Spoon into greased muffin cups and bake until done. Let muffins stand 10 minutes, then turn them onto rack.

Bake at 400 degrees 20 minutes • Makes 24 muffins.

• Most muffins bake at 400 degrees, but adjust recipes to your own oven. If muffins brown too quickly, then turn your oven down to 375 or even 350.

East Coast Orange Cranberry Muffins

This is a symbiotic recipe from the American East Coast. The sweetness of Florida oranges brings flavor to the cranberries from Maine's bogs, and both flavors are complemented by delicious Georgia pecans.

1 small can frozen ORANGE CONCENTRATE
SUGAR

Prepare muffin pans by spraying with non-stick spray. Spoon one teaspoon frozen orange concentrate into each muffin tin, then sprinkle about one-half teaspoon sugar in each muffin tin over the orange concentrate. Set pans aside until ready to cover with batter.

2½ cups unbleached FLOUR   1 tsp. SODA
1/3 cup SUGAR   1 cup chopped PECANS
1 tsp. SALT   ZEST of 2 ORANGES
1 Tbsp. BAKING POWDER   (grated outer rind)

Mix together the flour, sugar, salt, baking powder, soda, pecans and orange zest in a large bowl.

1 cup canned whole berry   1 Tbsp. LEMON JUICE
   CRANBERRY SAUCE   2 EGGS
2/3 cup fresh ORANGE JUICE   ¼ cup SAFFLOWER OIL

Whisk together the cranberry sauce, orange and lemon juice, eggs and oil in a smaller bowl. Pour the moist ingredients into the dry ingredients and stir quickly to blend. Spoon into the prepared muffin tins filling three-fourths full. Bake on center shelf of preheated oven until brown.

After removing from the oven, allow to stand a few minutes, then turn pans upside down so muffins will be upside down on waxed paper. If some of the orange and sugar mixture is in the muffin pans, remove it with a spoon and add it to the muffins.

Bake at 375 degrees 25 to 28 minutes • Makes 15 muffins.

Georgia Peanut Muffins

A visit to Plains, Georgia, home of former President Jimmy Carter, inspired these unusual muffins. Peanuts—actually a legume, not a nut—are high in protein. When combined with grain (the flour in this recipe), they produce a power-packed, tasty snack.

2 cups FLOUR
4 tsp. BAKING POWDER
1½ tsp. SALT
½ cup BROWN SUGAR
1 cup PEANUTS (if using salted peanuts, omit salt from recipe)

2 Tbsp. BUTTER, melted
¼ cup PEANUT BUTTER
1 cup MILK
1 EGG, beaten
1 tsp. VANILLA

Mix together flour, baking powder, salt and sugar in a large bowl. Add peanuts. In another bowl blend melted butter with peanut butter, stirring until well mixed. Add milk, egg and vanilla. Add peanut butter and milk mixture to dry ingredients all at once, stirring quickly. Fill muffin tins three-fourths full and place in hot oven on a middle shelf. Bake until tester comes out clean.

Bake at 375 degrees 25-30 minutes • Makes 16 muffins.

Swiss Black Currant Seed Muffins

Swiss black currant jam and toasted sesame seeds make these muffins a delightful addition to tea. Serve with a variety of imported cheeses for a true European touch.

2 cups FLOUR
1/3 cup SUGAR
1 Tbsp. BAKING POWDER
½ tsp. SALT
1 EGG
1 cup MILK
¼ cup BUTTER, melted and cooled

1 tsp. VANILLA
1/3 cup BLACK CURRANT JELLY
2 Tbsp. toasted SESAME SEEDS (Toast in small frying pan on medium heat. Stir until brown.)

Combine flour, sugar, baking powder and salt in a large bowl and stir well. In another bowl whisk egg, milk, melted butter and vanilla. Pour into center of dry ingredients and mix for 10 seconds. Fill muffin pans one-half full. Spoon a dollop of jelly in center and cover with more batter until they are three-fourths full. Sprinkle tops with toasted sesame seeds. Bake until brown.

Bake at 375 degrees about 25 minutes • Makes 14 muffins.

Half-Moon Bay Pumpkin Bran Muffins

The annual pumpkin festival in Half-Moon Bay, California inspired these spicy, nutritious muffins, an original creation by Lyle Farrow, twice named Chef of the West.

2 cups FLOUR
½ tsp. SALT
2/3 cup SUGAR
2 tsp. BAKING POWDER
1 tsp. SODA
1 tsp. NUTMEG
1 tsp. CINNAMON
1 tsp. ALLSPICE

1 cup PECANS
1 cup RAISIN BRAN CEREAL
¾ cup BRAN
2 EGGS
2/3 cup MILK
½ cup BUTTER, melted
1 cup PUMPKIN PUREE

Mix together flour, salt, sugar, baking powder, soda and spices in a large bowl. Add pecans, raisin bran and bran. In another bowl whisk eggs, milk, melted butter and pumpkin together. Add to dry ingredients, stirring quickly. Fill muffin pans three-fourths full and bake.

Bake at 375 degrees 20-25 minutes • Makes 21 muffins.

Cairo Date Muffins

For centuries, date palms along the Nile and in the desert oases have given travelers a welcome respite from the blazing Egyptian sun. Sweet and delectable, dates provide quick energy on the long journey. These Cairo Date Muffins will refresh and sustain us in our daily caravan of activities.

1 cup boiling WATER
1 cup DATES, diced
½ cup BUTTER
2/3 cup SUGAR
1 EGG
1 tsp. VANILLA

2¼ cups FLOUR
¼ tsp. SALT
2 tsp. BAKING POWDER
1 tsp. SODA
½ cup WALNUTS or pecans

Pour boiling water over the dates, butter and sugar. Stir until butter is melted and sugar dissolved. Beat in one egg. Add vanilla. In another bowl, mix flour, salt, baking powder and soda. Add to liquid mixture along with nuts. Stir quickly. Fill muffin pans three-fourths full and bake on shelf in middle of oven to brown evenly.

Bake at 375 degrees 15-18 minutes • Makes 18 muffins.

Indian Lemon Chutney Muffins

Lemons and chutney are found in many Indian meals. Chutney, a mixture of raisins, fruit, garlic, shallots, mustard, brown sugar and vinegar, is a popular condiment. These Indian Lemon Chutney Muffins bring a unique flavor to afternoon tea, or serve them as a light dessert after a dinner of spicy hot curry.

2 cups unbleached FLOUR
¼ cup BROWN SUGAR
¼ cup white SUGAR
1 Tbsp. BAKING POWDER
1 tsp. SODA
¼ tsp. SALT
zest (grated outer rind) of
   2 LEMONS

½ cup chopped WALNUTS
½ cup RAISINS
½ cup COCONUT
2 EGGS
2 Tbsp. BUTTER, melted
juice of 1 LEMON and enough
   MILK to make 1 cup
1 small jar CHUTNEY

Sift together flour, sugar, brown sugar, baking powder, soda and salt. Stir in lemon zest, chopped walnuts, raisins and coconut. In another bowl, whisk eggs with melted butter, lemon juice and milk. Make a well in the dry ingredients and add the liquid, stirring no more than 10 seconds. Fill greased muffin tins one-third full. Put one teaspoonful of chutney in the center of each muffin, then cover with remaining batter. Bake until done.

Bake at 375 degrees 25-30 minutes • Makes 14 muffins.

• Your muffins will be lighter when you mix them together quickly and lightly, for this produces the best rising effect.

Main Course Muffins

Main course muffins add something special to any meal. Serve hot muffins along with vegetable soup or chili—the grains in the muffins combine with legumes or dairy products to produce complementary protein.

For centuries many peoples of the world have developed their cuisines with their own folk wisdom, an intuitive knowledge of food complementarity. Mexican food combines corn or flour tortillas with beans and cheese in enchiladas, tostadas and burritos. Italians serve pasta with fresh vegetable sauces, topped with lots of grated cheese. The Chinese and Japanese serve bean sprouts, tofu and rice in many delicious combinations. In the Southern United States, "soul food" combines greens and corn bread with beans or black-eyed peas.

We can make use of food complementarity and add international flavor to our meals by serving these delicious muffins.

Cheese Muffins

Combining grains and additional dairy products, cheese muffins are packed with protein. Try them with soups on cold winter days—or with a dinner salad in the summertime. They are also delicious as snacks the next day. Take them on picnics. Split them open to make miniature sandwiches.

Swiss Fondue Muffins

Blending the flavors of good Swiss cheese, nutmeg and brandy, Swiss Fondue Muffins are an exotic addition to any meal. For a real Swiss taste, try these muffins warm from the oven with crisp apples, smoked ham or sausage.

2 cups all-purpose FLOUR
3 tsp. BAKING POWDER
1 Tbsp. SUGAR
½ tsp. NUTMEG
¼ tsp. GARLIC SALT
¼ tsp. SALT
1 cup grated SWISS,
   Emmentaler or Gruyere
   cheese

1 EGG
1 cup MILK
3 Tbsp. melted BUTTER or
   margarine
3 Tbsp. BRANDY or Kirsch
1 tsp. BUTTER FLAVORING

Mix together the flour, baking powder, sugar and spices. Blend in the grated cheese and mix well. In another bowl, whisk egg, milk, melted butter, brandy and butter flavoring. Make a well in the dry ingredients and add the egg and milk mixture, mixing quickly and lightly. Spoon into greased muffin cups. Sprinkle nutmeg on top of each muffin. Bake until tester comes out clean.

Bake at 350 degrees 25 to 30 minutes • Makes 10-12 muffins.

Welsh Rarebit Muffins

Welsh rarebit—toasted cheese on bread—is a main course in Wales. Try Welsh Rarebit Muffins hot from the oven, or split them open and toast lightly in the broiler.

1½ cups all-purpose FLOUR
½ cup RYE FLOUR
3 Tbsp. SUGAR
2 tsp. BAKING POWDER
½ tsp. SODA
½ tsp. SALT
1⅔ cups grated sharp
    CHEDDAR CHEESE

6 Tbsp. VEGETABLE OIL
2/3 cup SOUR CREAM
½ cup MILK
1 EGG
1½ tsp. WORCESTERSHIRE
    SAUCE

Mix first seven ingredients thoroughly in a large bowl. Whisk oil, sour cream, milk, egg and Worcestershire sauce in another bowl. Blend quickly with dry ingredients. Batter will be very lumpy. Spoon into muffin tins to three-fourths full. Bake until brown.

Bake at 400 degrees 20 minutes • Makes 15 muffins.

Wisconsin Cheddar Muffins

The heart of America's dairy country, Wisconsin, provides many cheese products. Try Wisconsin Cheddar Muffins along with a meal or as a light snack with apples and beer.

2 cups cake FLOUR
3 tsp. BAKING POWDER
1 Tbsp. SUGAR
½ tsp. SALT

½ cup grated CHEDDAR
    CHEESE
1 EGG
1 cup MILK
3 Tbsp. melted BUTTER

Stir together flour, baking powder, sugar and salt in a large bowl. Add the cheddar cheese and mix well. In another bowl, combine and beat well the egg, milk and melted butter. Blend the egg mixture together with the dry ingredients, mixing only until moistened. Spoon into greased muffin cups and bake until brown.

Bake at 350 degrees 25 minutes • Makes 12 muffins.

Corn Muffins

The early American colonists learned to make corn bread from the Indians, and since then corn has formed the basis for many American recipes. Corn meal muffins are an excellent accompaniment to any meal, especially useful for combined protein when beans are served.

Corn bread is a staple in many regional cuisines from Mexico to the Caribbean. Try some of our Tex-Mex Muffins along with a bowl of chili to spice up your next dinner. Enjoy our Puerto Rican Corn Muffins with any number of dishes. Both combine corn meal with cheese for extra protein.

New Mexico Blue Corn Muffins

Blue corn, or *maíz azul*, is a native Southwest food, cultivated for centuries by the Pueblo Indians along the Rio Grande in what is now New Mexico. It has long been part of native American tradition and religious ceremonies. *Harina maíz azul*, blue corn meal, is now available in many health food stores. Start your own tradition by serving these New Mexico Blue Corn Muffins with chili, gazpacho and other spicy Southwest dishes.

1½ cups BLUE CORN MEAL
½ cup unbleached FLOUR
3 tsp. BAKING POWDER
1 tsp. SODA
¼ tsp. SALT

2 EGGS
1 Tbsp. HONEY
1 Tbsp. OIL
1 cup BUTTERMILK

Mix together blue corn meal, flour, baking powder, soda and salt in a large bowl. In another bowl, whisk eggs with honey, oil and buttermilk. Make a well in the dry ingredients and quickly stir in the liquid, stirring not more than 10 seconds. Batter will be thin. Spoon into greased muffin tins and bake until lightly brown. Muffins will be crusty on the outside, tender and blue inside. Serve warm with butter.

Bake at 375 degrees 18-20 minutes • Makes 15 muffins.

Indian Corn Muffins

Indian Corn Muffins are a hearty accompaniment to soups, spicy bean dishes or salads. They are also delicious with cheese.

2 cups CORNMEAL
½ cup whole wheat
   pastry FLOUR
1 tsp. BAKING POWDER
½ tsp. BAKING SODA

2 large EGGS, beaten
2 cups BUTTERMILK
1 Tbsp. HONEY
1 Tbsp. OIL

Stir together the cornmeal, flour, baking powder and soda in a large bowl. Whisk eggs, buttermilk, honey and oil in another bowl. Combine the two just until mixed. Spoon into greased muffin cups and bake until done.

Bake at 375 degrees 20 to 25 minutes • Makes 12 muffins.

Jalapeño Corn Muffins

Tangy jalapeno jelly and cream cheese are the surprise centers of these delicious corn muffins. Serve with a Mexican dinner of enchiladas or chile rellenos and refried beans. Also good as miniature muffins for hors d'oeuvres.

2 cups CORN MEAL
½ cup whole wheat
   pastry FLOUR
1½ tsp. BAKING POWDER
1 tsp. SODA
2 EGGS

2 cups BUTTERMILK
1 Tbsp. HONEY
1 Tbsp. OIL
½ cup JALAPEÑO JELLY
½ cup CREAM CHEESE

Stir together corn meal, flour, baking powder and soda. In another bowl, whisk eggs, buttermilk, honey and oil. Make a well in the dry ingredients and add the liquid, stirring for no more than 10 seconds. Put one tablespoon batter into greased muffin tins. Then add about one teaspoon each cream cheese and jalapeño jelly. Cover with batter until muffin tins are two-thirds full. Bake until done. Olé!

Bake at 375 degrees 20-25 minutes • Makes 16 muffins.

Kentucky Hush Puppy Muffins

A family recipe for another southern favorite inspired these muffins. Golden, hot, and flavored with chopped onions and just a hint of tomato, Kentucky Hush Puppy muffins are especially good with seafood.

2 cups CORNMEAL
½ cup whole wheat
    pastry FLOUR
1 tsp. BAKING POWDER
½ tsp. BAKING SODA
½ tsp. SALT
1 med. ONION, chopped

2 slices BACON, fried and
    chopped (optional)
2 large EGGS, beaten
1 Tbsp. OIL
1 Tbsp. HONEY
1¼ cups BUTTERMILK
3 Tbsp. TOMATO SAUCE

Stir together cornmeal, flour, baking powder, soda and salt in a large bowl. Mix in the chopped onion (and bacon pieces, if desired). Whisk eggs, oil, honey, buttermilk and tomato sauce in another bowl. Combine the two just until mixed. Spoon into greased muffin cups and bake until tops begin to turn golden brown.

Bake at 375 degress 20 to 25 minutes • Makes 12 muffins.

Mexican Corn Muffins

Bright, colorful and tasty, Mexican Corn Muffins are perfect with soup or chili. They're also delicious for breakfast with maple syrup and sausages.

½ cup BUTTER, melted
1¼ cups BUTTERMILK
2 EGGS
1 cup FLOUR
1 cup CORNMEAL,
    finely-ground

½ tsp. SALT
½ cup SUGAR
3 tsp. BAKING POWDER
1 tsp. BAKING SODA
1 can MEXICORN,
    well drained

In a small bowl, whisk melted butter, buttermilk and eggs well. In large bowl, sift together the flour, cornmeal, salt, sugar, baking powder, soda and drained Mexicorn. Quickly stir buttermilk mixture into dry ingredients. Batter will be lumpy. Spoon into greased muffin tins filling three-fourths full. Bake until brown.

Bake at 400 degrees 20 to 25 minutes • Makes 20 muffins.

Bourbon Corn Muffins

Kentucky bourbon whiskey is the special ingredient in these unusual muffins. They're delicious with stewed chicken and home-made noodles, or try them for brunch with hot syrup, southern ham or sausage.

1½ cups coarse CORN MEAL
1½ cups BUTTERMILK
¼ cup BOURBON WHISKEY
1/3 cup BROWN SUGAR
1 tsp. SALT

Combine all ingredients and let stand one hour to soak corn meal.

2 large EGGS
1½ cups unbleached FLOUR
1 tsp. SODA
1½ tsp. BAKING POWDER
¼ cup BUTTER, melted

Whisk the two eggs and add to the cornmeal mixture. In another bowl, sift together flour, soda and baking powder. Stir into corn meal mixture. Add melted butter, stirring quickly, and spoon into greased muffin tins. Bake until done and enjoy while still warm.

Bake at 400 degrees 15 minutes • Makes 18 muffins.

Southern Cornbread Muffins

Try Southern Cornbread Muffins along with a traditional dinner of fried chicken and green beans or serve with ham hocks and blackeyed peas.

1/3 cup SHORTENING
1/3 cup SUGAR (reduce sugar
   if you do not like your cornbread too sweet)
1¼ cups MILK
1 beaten EGG
1 cup FLOUR
½ tsp. SALT
4 tsp. BAKING POWDER
1 cup CORNMEAL

Cream shortening and sugar together. Add milk and egg. Add flour, salt and baking powder. Add cornmeal, stirring just enough to mix. Spoon into greased muffin tins and bake until done.

Bake at 425 degrees 25 minutes • Makes 12 muffins.

Tex-Mex Muffins

Combining chile peppers with cheese, Tex-Mex Muffins are hot and spicy. Serve them with chili or burritos and a salad of tomatoes, lettuce and guacamole.

2 cups CORN MEAL
½ cup whole wheat
  pastry FLOUR
1 tsp. BAKING POWDER
½ tsp. BAKING SODA
1 tsp. CUMIN
2 EGGS, beaten
1 Tbsp. HONEY

1 Tbsp. OIL
2 cups BUTTERMILK
1 cup JALAPEÑO CHEESE
  (or one cup cheddar cheese
  with 1-2 Tbsp. chopped
  jalapeño peppers, to taste)
½ cup chopped CHILES

Stir together corn meal, flour, baking powder, soda and cumin. Beat eggs and add honey, oil and buttermilk. Make a well in the dry ingredients and quickly add the wet ingredients. Fold in cheese and chiles. Batter will be lumpy. Spoon into greased muffin tins and bake until muffins begin to brown and pull away from the sides of the tin. Test with toothpick, which should come out clean.

Bake at 375 degrees 20 to 25 minutes • Makes 12 muffins.

Puerto Rican Corn Muffins

Surullitos, Puerto Rican cornmeal and cheese sticks, inspired these tasty muffins, perfect with soups or salads. Try them with black bean soup, a Caribbean favorite, or any number of spicy dishes.

2 cups CORN MEAL
½ cup whole wheat
  pastry FLOUR
1 tsp. BAKING POWDER
½ tsp. SODA
½ to 1 tsp. fresh ground
  BLACK PEPPER (to taste)

1 cup grated mild
  CHEDDAR CHEESE
2 EGGS, beaten
1 Tbsp. HONEY
1 Tbsp. OIL
2 cups BUTTERMILK

Mix together corn meal, flour, baking powder, soda and pepper. Blend in grated cheese. In another bowl, whisk eggs, honey, oil and buttermilk. Make a well in the dry ingredients and quickly stir in liquid mixture. Spoon into greased muffin cups and bake until tester comes out clean.

Bake at 375 degrees 20 to 25 minutes • Makes 12 muffins.

A miscellany
of main course muffins...

Minnesota Wild Rice Muffins

Wild rice grew in many of the 10,000 lakes in Minnesota and was harvested by Indians in canoes long before the white man came. Unlike regular rice, wild rice grows in cold climates. Its new shoots rise out of the lakes in early spring and must still be harvested in small boats, which makes it a rare and costly treat. Try these savory wild rice muffins instead of dressing with your next chicken dinner.

1 cup all-purpose
  unbleached FLOUR
1 cup whole wheat FLOUR
1 Tbsp. SUGAR
4 tsp. BAKING POWDER
1 tsp. SODA
1 tsp. SALT
1 tsp. minced ONION FLAKES

1 tsp. SAGE
½ tsp. THYME
1 cup cooked WILD RICE
  well drained
  (directions below)*
2 EGGS
1½ cups BUTTERMILK
1/3 cup melted BUTTER

Combine the first ten ingredients in a large mixing bowl. Whisk the eggs, buttermilk and melted shortening in another bowl. Combine quickly, pouring the wet ingredients into the dry. Spoon into greased muffin tins. Bake until done and serve warm.

Bake at 375 degrees 22-25 minutes • Makes 14 muffins.

*Wild rice needs to be washed by putting a cupful in a large pan of cold water. The chaff will rise to the top and can be poured off as more water is added. If the rice has not been processed, check carefully for small pebbles. Bring water to a boil, add the wild rice with a dash of salt, if desired. Lower the heat and cook until the white part of the rice puffs out. If not cooked enough, it will be hard and sharp to the tongue.

Polish Onion Muffins

Inspired by Polish onion biscuits, these savory muffins are great with a hearty bowl of homemade soup. Serve them with *krupnik* (barley-potato soup) or *grochowka* (split pea soup) for a real Polish flavor.

1½ cups FLOUR	1 EGG
1 tsp. SUGAR	2 Tbsp. BUTTER, melted
1½ tsp. BAKING POWDER	1 cup BUTTERMILK
½ tsp. SODA	¼ cup grated ONION
½ tsp. SALT	1 Tbsp. melted BUTTER
½ tsp. DILL	1 Tbsp. POPPY SEEDS

Mix together flour, sugar, baking powder, soda, salt and dill. Whisk egg with buttermilk, two tablespoons melted butter and grated onion. Blend with dry ingredients, stirring no more than ten seconds. Spoon into greased muffin tins. Brush tops with one tablespoon melted butter and sprinkle with poppy seeds. Bake until golden.

Bake at 400 degrees 15-20 minutes • Makes 10 muffins.

Colonial Applejack Muffins

Applejack was first developed in Monmouth, New Jersey by William Laird in 1698. In 1760, George Washington obtained the secret recipe and introduced it into the Virginia Colony. These Colonial Applejack Muffins will add a special touch to meals or teatime.

2 cups unbleached FLOUR	4 tsp. BAKING POWDER
1 cup dark BROWN SUGAR	1 tsp. SODA
1½ cups grated, unpeeled	1 tsp. CINNAMON
GREEN APPLES	2 EGGS
1 cup chopped WALNUTS	½ cup APPLEJACK LIQUOR
1 tsp. SALT	¼ cup melted BUTTER

Blend the first eight ingredients in a large mixing bowl. Whisk eggs, applejack and butter in a small bowl. Make a well in the center of dry ingredients and pour in the egg mixture. Stir quickly until blended. Spoon into muffin tins, filling to the top. Bake in preheated oven until brown on top to be sure the apples are cooked. Delicious and nutritious any time of the day.

Bake at 375 degrees 15-18 minutes • Makes 16 muffins.

Bara Brith Muffins

Adapted from a recipe for *bara brith*, Welsh brown bread studded with raisins and currants, these muffins are a special accompaniment to dinner or a welcome snack any time with fruit or cheese, preferably Welsh *caerphilly*.

1 cup unbleached FLOUR
2/3 cup whole wheat
   pastry FLOUR
¼ cup BROWN SUGAR
2 tsp. BAKING POWDER
1 tsp. SODA
½ tsp. NUTMEG

½ cup RAISINS or sultanas
1 cup CURRANTS
1 EGG
2 Tbsp. BUTTER, melted
½ cup TEA
½ cup BUTTERMILK
1 Tbsp. MOLASSES

Mix together flour, wheat flour, brown sugar, baking powder, soda and nutmeg. Mix in raisins and currants. In another bowl whisk egg with melted butter, tea, buttermilk and molasses. Quickly add wet to dry ingredients, stirring 10 seconds. Spoon into greased muffin tins and bake until done.

Bake at 400 degrees 15-20 minutes • Makes 12 muffins.

Yugoslavian Potato Muffins

Root crops, potatoes and carrots, carefully stored in cellars helped people survive the long dark European winters. Creative cooks throughout Yugoslavia, Germany and the Scandinavian countries developed potato breads, dumplings and delicious potato pancakes, which inspired these Yugoslavian Potato Muffins, perfect with soup or salad for a light meal.

2 cups unbleached FLOUR
4 tsp. BAKING POWDER
1½ tsp. SALT
2 tsp. dried ONION FLAKES
1 Tbsp. SUGAR
1 tsp. CARAWAY SEEDS

2 EGGS
1 cup unsweetened
   APPLESAUCE
6 Tbsp. melted BUTTER
1½ cups grated, raw
   white POTATOES

Blend the first six ingredients in a large mixing bowl. Whisk the eggs, applesauce, melted butter and grated potatoes in a small bowl. Pour into flour mixture, stirring quickly. Spoon into greased muffin tins. Bake until brown. Serve warm with butter or honey.

Bake at 375 degrees 25 minutes or until brown • Makes 12 muffins.

Chinese Vegetable Muffins

Water chestnuts, rice, green onions, pineapple, ground ginger and hoisin—plum sauce—add traditional Chinese flavor to these tasty main course muffins. Serve with a Mandarin or Szechuan main course or with a salad for a light meal. A special treat for summer luncheons.

2½ cups unbleached FLOUR
2 Tbsp. SUGAR
4 tsp. BAKING POWDER
1 tsp. SODA
½ tsp. SALT
2/3 cup cooked, white RICE, cooled
½ cup sliced GREEN ONION
2 EGGS
reserved PINEAPPLE JUICE (about ½ cup) and enough BUTTERMILK to make 1 cup

3 Tbsp. melted BUTTER
1½ tsp. fresh, ground GINGER
¾ cup sliced WATER CHESTNUTS, chopped and drained
1 cup PINEAPPLE TIDBITS, well drained (reserve ½ cup of the liquid to add to buttermilk, above)
1 small jar CHINESE PLUM SAUCE

Mix together flour, sugar, baking powder, soda and salt. Stir in cooked white rice and sliced green onion. In another bowl, whisk eggs with resrved pineapple juice and buttermilk, melted butter, and ground ginger. Stir in chopped water chestnuts and pineapple chunks. Make a well in the dry ingredients and quickly add the moist ingredients, stirring not more than 10 seconds. Batter will be lumpy. Spoon into greased muffin tins, filling two-thirds full and topping each muffin with a teaspoon of plum sauce. Bake until done.

Bake at 400 degrees 15 to 20 minutes • Makes 16 muffins.

• If all the muffin tins are not full, pour water into the empty ones. This will not only save the muffin pans, but will add moisture to the oven and enlarge the muffins while baking.

Bavarian Apple Sausage Muffins

Inspired by *Himmel und Erde*, the delicious apple, onion, pork and potato dish of southern Germany, these muffins are perfect with a hearty bowl of soup for a light winter meal. Or enjoy them as a snack with a slab of good cheese, pickles and beer.

1¼ cups unbleached FLOUR
½ cup RYE FLOUR
1 Tbsp. BROWN SUGAR
3 tsp. BAKING POWDER
1 tsp. SODA
½ tsp. fresh ground PEPPER
½ tsp. ALLSPICE
½ tsp. CELERY SEED
½ cup raw, grated POTATO
1/3 cup diced raw ONION

1 tsp. CIDER VINEGAR
1 cup diced raw APPLES
¾ cup cooked, drained
  GERMAN SAUSAGE (or
  uncooked soy sausage),
  sliced
2 EGGS
1 Tbsp. SHERRY
3 Tbsp. melted BUTTER
1 cup BUTTERMILK

Mix together flour, rye flour, sugar, baking powder, soda and spices. In a small bowl, sprinkle grated potato and onions with one teaspoon cider vinegar. Stir grated potato, onions, chopped apples and sausages into dry ingredients. In another bowl, whisk eggs with sherry, melted butter and buttermilk. Make a well and add liquid ingredients, stirring not more than 10 seconds. Batter will be lumpy. Fill greased muffin cups with batter and bake until lightly browned.

Bake at 375 degrees 20-22 minutes • Makes 16 muffins.

Finnish Cranberry Muffins

Inspired by *Ilmapuuro*, a Finnish cranberry pudding. Try Finnish Cranberry Muffins along with a traditional smorgasbord or any holiday feast. They are also good with tea.

2 cups cake FLOUR or
  1¾ cups all-purpose flour
½ tsp. SALT
1/3 cup SUGAR
2 tsp. BAKING POWDER

2 EGGS
¾ cup MILK
¼ cup melted BUTTER
1 cup chopped CRANBERRIES
1 tsp. grated ORANGE rind

Combine flour, salt, sugar and baking powder, sifting well. Blend eggs, milk and butter and pour into center well of dry ingredients. Mix only until moistened. Fold in the cranberries and grated orange rind. Spoon into greased muffin cups and bake until done.

Bake at 400 degrees 20 to 25 minutes • Makes 18 muffins.

German Cabbage Muffins

Like their Scandinavian and Slavic neighbors, Germans love cabbage. They prepare it in a variety of ways from cabbage soups and cabbage salads to their pungent sauerkraut. Try these German Cabbage Muffins with a bowl of steaming soup or serve for lunch along with sausage and salad. Wunderbar!

1¾ cups unbleached FLOUR
1 Tbsp. BAKING POWDER
1 tsp. SALT
1 Tbsp. SUGAR
2 tsp. ONION FLAKES

2 tsp. CELERY SEED
2 full cups grated CABBAGE
2 EGGS
¾ cup low-fat MILK
6 Tbsp. melted BUTTER

Combine flour, baking powder, salt, sugar, onion flakes and celery seed thoroughly. Add the grated cabbage and stir into these dry ingredients. Whisk the eggs, milk and melted butter together well. Add to dry ingredients and stir quickly, making sure it isn't over 10 seconds. Spoon into greased muffin pans and bake in preheated oven until done.

Bake at 400 degrees 20 minutes • Makes 12 muffins.

Scandinavian Dill Potato Muffins

Dill is a favorite herb throughout Scandinavia. Serve these dill muffins instead of potatoes or with pickled herring and an assortment of cheeses for a true Nordic taste.

2 cups all-purpose FLOUR
1½ tsp. BAKING POWDER
¼ tsp. SODA
½ tsp. SALT
3 Tbsp. fresh DILL or
   1 tsp. dried dill
2 EGGS, beaten

½ cup SOUR CREAM
2/3 cup mashed POTATOES
¾ cup MILK
½ tsp. BUTTER FLAVORING
¼ cup BUTTER or
   margarine, melted

Stir together flour, baking powder, soda, salt and dill. In another bowl, whisk eggs and stir in sour cream, mashed potatoes, milk, butter flavoring and melted shortening. Make a well in the dry ingredients and quickly add the egg-milk mixture. Batter will be sticky. Spoon into greased muffin cups and sprinkle extra dill on top of each muffin. Bake until tops begin to turn golden and tester comes out clean.

Bake at 400 degrees 20 minutes • Makes 12 muffins.

South American Quinoa Muffins

Quinoa, (pronounced keen-wa), the sacred grain of the Incas, has the highest and most complete protein content of all the world's grains. It remains the staple food for millions of South American Indians. With its delicate, nutty taste, protein, B complex and vitamin E, it is becoming increasingly popular in North America. *Quinoa* can now be found in many health food stores. These South American Quinoa Muffins with their light texture and subtle flavor will add a nutritious boost to meal or snack time.

1 cup whole wheat FLOUR
½ cup unbleached FLOUR
3 Tbsp. BROWN SUGAR
1 Tbsp. BAKING POWDER
1 tsp. SODA
½ tsp. SALT

½ cup CURRANTS
1 cup cooked QUINOA*
2 EGGS
2 Tbsp. melted BUTTER
1 cup BUTTERMILK

Sift together flours, brown sugar, baking powder, soda and salt. Stir in currants and cooked quinoa. In another bowl, whisk eggs with melted butter and buttermilk. Make a well in dry ingredients and add liquid, stirring no more than 10 seconds. Spoon into greased muffin tins and bake until golden brown.

Bake at 400 degrees 18-20 minutes • Makes 12 muffins.

*To prepare quinoa, first rinse thoroughly to remove saponins (a soapy coating on the outside). Then place in a large saucepan, using two cups water to one cup quinoa. Bring to a boil, then reduce heat to simmer for 10 to 15 minutes until all the water is absorbed. The grain will turn translucent, and the outer germ ring will separate. Use as you would any grain.

Swedish Lingonberry Muffins

Lingonberries are popular throughout Scandinavia, served fresh, baked in delicious fruit breads, or enjoyed in sparkling jams and jellies. Try these muffins with the traditional smorgasbord or as a special accompaniment to any meal.

1 cup LINGONBERRIES   3 Tbsp. SUGAR

Sprinkle fresh lingonberries with sugar and let stand while measuring the other ingredients. If canned lingonberries are used, leave out the sugar and just measure one cup of the canned berries, since they are already sweetened.

2 cups all-purpose FLOUR   1 EGG, well beaten
3 tsp. BAKING POWDER   1 cup MILK
½ tsp. SALT   2 Tbsp. melted BUTTER

Mix flour, baking powder and salt in a large bowl. Combine egg, milk, butter in another bowl and pour into well in center of dry ingredients. Stir lightly and quickly fold in berries. Batter will be lumpy. Fill muffin cups three-fourths full and bake until tester comes out clean.
    Bake at 400 to 425 degrees 20 to 25 minutes • Makes 12 muffins.

Southern Corn Fritter Muffins

Hot corn fritters are a mealtime favorite in the American south. These Corn Fritter Muffins are a lower cholesterol variation. Serve them as a main course accompaniment or with maple syrup for a special brunch.

1½ cups all-purpose FLOUR   1 cup canned CORN, drained
2 Tbsp. SUGAR   1 EGG
1½ tsp. BAKING POWDER   2 Tbsp. BUTTER or
½ tsp. SODA   margarine, melted
pinch SALT   1¼ cups BUTTERMILK

Mix flour, sugar, baking powder, soda and salt together in a large bowl. Stir in canned corn. Whisk egg, melted butter and buttermilk. Add quickly to dry ingredients. Spoon batter into greased muffin cups and bake until lightly browned.
    Bake at 400 degrees 15-20 minutes • Makes 10 muffins.

Gilroy Garlic Muffins

Every year visitors flock to the small northern California town known as the "garlic capital of the world" for the Gilroy Garlic Festival. During harvest time the odor of garlic fills the air for miles around, calling garlic lovers together to share recipes, sample hundreds of garlic dishes, and drink a unique garlic wine. Inspired by the festival, these Gilroy Garlic Muffins are guaranteed to liven up your meals.

2 cups FLOUR
4 tsp. BAKING POWDER
½ cup ROMANO CHEESE
½ tsp. SALT
1 Tbsp. SUGAR
1 cup MILK
1 large EGG

3 Tbsp. melted BUTTER
1 Tbsp. GARLIC OIL*
2 cloves diced fresh GARLIC
½ cup diced
    GREEN ONION tops
¼ cup (2 oz.) diced PIMIENTOS
½ cup sliced green OLIVES
    (optional)

Measure first five (dry) ingredients and combine thoroughly in a large mixing bowl. Measure the next five ingredients and combine in blender on high speed until garlic is thoroughly chopped. Add the green onions, pimientos and olives to the dry mixture in the bowl. Add the wet ingredients and stir not over 10 seconds to combine. Fill greased muffin tins three-fourths full and bake for about 20 minutes or until tops are lightly browned.

Bake at 375 degrees about 20 minutes • Makes 14 muffins.

*Peel garlic cloves and put into a pint jar. Cover cloves with salad oil or olive oil. You will not only have garlic cloves readily available for use in the refrigerator, but garlic oil for baking.

Finnish Carrot Rice Muffins

Porkkanalaatikko, a popular carrot rice casserole in Finland, inspired these Finnish Carrot Rice Muffins. Their delicate flavor will add interest to any meal. Serve with dill butter (creamed butter with dill) for an authentic Finnish touch.

1½ cups all-purpose FLOUR
1 Tbsp. BROWN SUGAR
½ tsp. SALT
2 tsp. BAKING POWDER
1 cup shredded CARROT
½ cup cooked RICE

2 EGGS, beaten
1 cup MILK
½ tsp. BUTTER FLAVORING
2 Tbsp. BUTTER, melted
½ cup WHEAT GERM

Mix together flour, sugar, salt and baking powder. Add shredded carrots and rice and blend together well. In another bowl, whisk eggs with milk, butter flavoring and melted butter. Make a well in the dry ingredients and add liquid ingredients, stirring quickly. Spoon into greased muffin cups and sprinkle tops with wheat germ. Bake until lightly brown and tester comes out clean.

Bake at 400 degrees 20-25 minutes • Makes 12 muffins.

West African Yam Muffins

Yams are essential to the West African diet, served throughout Nigeria and Liberia in chips, balls, fritters, soups, stews, sauces and yam pone, the basis for this muffin recipe. Serve West African Yam Muffins with rice, bananas and beans or ground nuts (peanuts) for an authentic African taste.

1½ cups all-purpose FLOUR
1 Tbsp. BAKING POWDER
½ tsp. SALT
1 tsp. ground GINGER
¼ cup BROWN SUGAR
2 EGGS

½ cup YAMS, cooked
   and mashed
2/3 cup MILK
3 Tbsp. BUTTER or
   margarine, melted
1-2 Tbsp. MOLASSES (to taste)

Blend together flour, baking powder, salt, ginger and brown sugar in a large bowl. Whisk eggs, yam, milk, butter and molasses. Make a well in the dry ingredients and add the liquid mixture, stirring lightly and quickly. Spoon into greased muffin cups and bake until tester comes out clean.

Bake at 400 degrees 20 to 25 minutes • Makes 10 muffins.

Mediterranean Herb Muffins

In the sunlit lands of the Mediterranean, fresh herbs enhance the taste of evening meals, and every self-respecting cook has fresh herbs growing in the garden or on a sunny window sill. These Mediterranean Herb Muffins, flavored with fresh herbs and grated Parmesan cheese, will fill your kitchen with a delightful aroma and add a special zest to mealtime.

1½ cups all-purpose FLOUR
1 Tbsp. SUGAR
1½ tsp. BAKING POWDER
½ tsp. SODA
pinch SALT
1 tsp. GARLIC POWDER
1/3 cup grated
   PARMESAN CHEESE

½ cup finely-chopped
   fresh HERBS
   (oregano or basil)
1 EGG
2 Tbsp. BUTTER, melted
1¼ cups BUTTERMILK

Sift together flour, sugar, baking powder, soda, salt and garlic powder. Stir in Parmesan cheese and fresh herbs. In another bowl, whisk egg with melted butter and buttermilk. Add to dry ingredients, mixing for only 10 seconds. Spoon into greased muffin cups and bake until done.

Bake at 400 degrees 15 to 20 minutes • Makes 12 muffins.

BASIL

• Be sure your herbs and spices are fresh. All spices lose their potency after a while, and tired spices produce tired tasting muffins.

Italian Pizza Muffins

With the first bite, Italian Pizza Muffins greet you with the flavor of Italy. Serve them with assorted cheeses and salami for a light snack, or let them add life to any meal. Molto bene!

2 cups all-purpose FLOUR
¼ cup grated
    PARMESAN CHEESE
1 Tbsp. SUGAR
2 tsp. BAKING POWDER
1 tsp. SODA
½ cup chopped GREEN ONIONS
¼ cup SALAMI or
    cooked Italian sausage
1/3 cup sliced pimiento-
    stuffed green OLIVES

¼ cup minced oil-packed,
    sun-dried TOMATOES,
    drained
1 tsp. FENNEL SEED
1 med. GARLIC clove, crushed
½ tsp. OREGANO
2 EGGS
½ cup OLIVE OIL
1/3 cup MILK
1/3 cup SOUR CREAM

Mix dry ingredients (first five) in a large bowl. Stir in green onions, salami or sausage, olives, tomatoes and spices. Mix thoroughly. In another bowl, beat eggs, oil, milk and sour cream. Add this to a well in the bowl of dry ingredients. Stir quickly. Batter will be lumpy. Fill muffin cups three-fourths full. Bake until brown.

Bake at 400 degrees 20 minutes • Makes 16 muffins.

Irish Soda Muffins

Our version of traditional Irish soda bread, these muffins are perfect with corned beef and cabbage, Irish stews or any time you'd like to add "a touch of the Irish" to your meal.

2 cups all-purpose FLOUR
1 tsp. SODA
½ tsp. SALT

2 tsp. SUGAR
1½ cups BUTTERMILK
¼ cup BUTTER, melted

Mix together flour, soda, salt and sugar. In another bowl, whisk together buttermilk and melted butter. Add to dry ingredients, mixing quickly. Batter will be stiff. Spoon into greased muffin cups and bake until tops are golden brown.

Bake at 400 degrees 15 to 20 minutes • Makes 10-12 muffins.

Norwegian Whole Wheat Muffins

Hearty Norwegian *Hvetekake* inspired these tasty whole wheat muffins. We added walnuts for extra crunch. Try them for a delicious accompaniment to meals. Or serve with cream cheese for a light snack.

1 cup whole wheat FLOUR
1 cup unbleached white FLOUR
½ tsp. SALT
1 Tbsp. BAKING POWDER
1 tsp. SODA

½ cup BROWN SUGAR
1 cup coarsely-chopped
  WALNUTS
1 cup BUTTERMILK
2 beaten EGGS
1/3 cup melted BUTTER

Sift together whole wheat and unbleached flour, salt, baking powder and sugar in a large bowl. Stir in nuts. In another bowl combine buttermilk, eggs and shortening and pour into a well in center of dry ingredients. Stir until moistened. Spoon into greased muffin cups and bake until done.

Bake at 425 degrees 15 minutes • Makes 18 muffins.

Yankee Economy Muffins

Yankee ingenuity and frugality helped Americans settle a vast continent and make it through the Depression. Apply Yankee ingenuity to your muffin making and turn leftovers into these delicious muffins.

2 cups FLOUR
1 Tbsp. BAKING POWDER
½ tsp. SALT
1 cup cooked RICE
  (or left-over oatmeal)
½ cup RAISINS

½ cup BROWN SUGAR
1¼ cups MILK
2 EGG YOLKS
2 Tbsp. melted BUTTER
2 EGG WHITES beaten
  until stiff

Measure first five ingredients and mix well in a large bowl. Whisk brown sugar, milk, yolks and butter in a smaller bowl. Make a well in the center of the first five dry ingredients and pour in the whisked ingredients from the small bowl. Mix quickly, add beaten egg whites and spoon into muffin tins.

Bake at 400 degrees 20 minutes • Makes 18 muffins.

Recipe Notes

Muffins for Dessert

Muffins make wonderful desserts. Either by themselves or with fresh fruit or ice cream, they are sure to please. Next time, instead of Cherries Jubilee, serve your guests French Brandied Cherry Muffins, exotic Pina Colada Muffins, or some of our irresistible chocolate muffins.

Chocolate Muffins

Do you find chocolate absolutely irresistible? Try our chocolate muffins—dark, bittersweet New York Chocolate Cheesecake, New England Toll House, Chocolate Mousse and more—a chocolate lover's paradise!

Central American Cocoa Muffins

Indigenous to Central and South America, cocoa was used by the Aztecs and Mayans in religious rites. The Aztec drink of ground cocoa beans was thought to be an aphrodisiac by Montezuma. Sixteenth century Spanish explorers introduced cocoa to Europe, and chocolate soon became an international sensation. Prized for its quick energy boost, chocolate has been taken on space missions by U.S. astronauts. Enjoy these Central American Cocoa Muffins for your own chocolate sensation.

1½ cups unbleached FLOUR
1/3 cup unsweetened COCOA
1½ tsp. BAKING POWDER
½ tsp. SODA
½ cup SUGAR
½ cup chopped WALNUTS

1 EGG
2 Tbsp. melted BUTTER
1⅛ cups BUTTERMILK
1 tsp. VANILLA
sliced ALMONDS

Mix flour, cocoa, baking powder, soda and sugar. Add chopped walnuts. In another bowl whisk egg with melted butter, buttermilk and vanilla. Quickly stir into dry ingredients. Spoon batter into greased muffin tins. Top with sliced almonds. Bake until done.

Bake at 400 degrees 15-20 minutes • Makes 12 muffins.

Johnny Appleseed Fudge Muffins

These applesauce chocolate muffins were inspired by Johnny Appleseed, the famous ancestor of Gen's friend Fay Weisler. In the early 1800s, John Chapman, who became known as Johnny Appleseed, wandered from Pennsylvania to Ohio, sowing apple seeds and becoming part of American history. Serve warm Johnny Appleseed Muffins with a bowl of fresh berries.

2 squares unsweetened
   CHOCOLATE
½ cup MARGARINE or butter
1 cup APPLESAUCE
2 EGGS
¾ cup BROWN SUGAR
SALT

1 tsp. VANILLA
1 cup FLOUR
½ cup chopped WALNUTS
¼ tsp. SODA
1 tsp. BAKING POWDER
CONFECTIONER'S SUGAR

Melt chocolate and butter. Combine the first seven ingredients in bowl, whisking until well blended. In another bowl mix together well the flour, nuts, soda and baking powder, then add all at once to the moist ingredients. Stir 10 seconds until blended. Spoon into prepared muffin pans and bake until done. Serve warm, sprinkled with confectioner's sugar.

Bake at 350 degrees 15 to 18 minutes • Makes 15 muffins.

• Let muffins stand a minute or two before removing from tins. They come out more easily that way. Often, you can simply turn the pan upside down over a board and the muffins fall right out. Sometimes you may have to help them out by running a knife along the side of each muffin cup.

Chocolate Mousse Muffins

Who can resist the taste of deep, dark chocolate? This muffin was inspired by French chocolate mousse and contains three different kinds of chocolate!

5 oz. semisweet CHOCOLATE
2 oz. unsweetened CHOCOLATE
½ cup BUTTER
¾ cup SOUR CREAM
2/3 cup BROWN SUGAR
¼ cup light CORN SYRUP

1 EGG
1 tsp. VANILLA
1½ cups all-purpose FLOUR
1 tsp. BAKING SODA
¼ tsp. SALT
2/3 cup CHOCOLATE CHIPS semi-sweet

Melt first three ingredients (chocolates and butter) in a double boiler. Whisk sour cream, sugar, syrup, egg and vanilla in a small bowl. Put remaining ingredients in large bowl with two-thirds cup chocolate chips and stir thoroughly. Add melted chocolate to mixture in small bowl. Pour into well in the large bowl of dry ingredients and blend for 10 seconds. Batter will be lumpy. Spoon into greased muffin pans until three-fourths full. Bake until tester comes out clean.

Bake at 400 degrees 20 minutes • Makes 14 muffins.

Schwarzwälder Kirsch Muffins

Inspired by the luscious German Black Forest cake, or *Schwarzwälder Kirschtorte*, filled with nuts and cherries, this is a muffin to remember!

4 oz. semisweet CHOCOLATE
1 oz. unsweetened CHOCOLATE
½ cup BUTTER
¾ cup SOUR CREAM
2/3 cup BROWN SUGAR
¼ cup light CORN SYRUP
1 EGG
1 tsp. VANILLA

1½ cups all-purpose FLOUR
1 tsp. BAKING SODA
¼ tsp. SALT
1 cup coarsely-chopped WALNUTS
1 cup diced BING CHERRIES, well drained

Melt chocolate with butter. Whisk cream, sugar, syrup, egg and vanilla. Mix flour, baking powder, salt, nuts and well-drained cherries. Add chocolate and butter mixture to eggs, cream, sugar and syrup. Pour into well of dry ingredients. Stir quickly. Spoon into muffin pans three-fourths full. Bake until tester comes out clean.

Bake at 375 degrees 20-25 minutes • Makes 16 muffins.

American
Rocky Road Muffins

As tasty as the ice cream of the same name, rocky road muffins are a great dessert on picnics, or serve with ice cream to complement their flavorful combination of chocolate, nuts and marshmallows.

4 oz. semisweet CHOCOLATE
1 oz. unsweetened CHOCOLATE
1/3 cup BUTTER
¾ cup SOUR CREAM
½ cup BROWN SUGAR
¼ cup light CORN SYRUP
1 EGG

1¼ tsp. VANILLA
1½ cups all-purpose FLOUR
¼ tsp. SALT
1 tsp. BAKING SODA
2/3 cup chopped WALNUTS
2/3 cup miniature
    MARSHMALLOWS

Melt first three ingredients (chocolates and butter) in a double boiler. Whisk the liquid ingredients (sour cream, sugar, syrup, egg and vanilla) in a small bowl. Put remaining ingredients in large bowl and stir thoroughly. Add melted chocolate to liquid mixture. Pour into well in large bowl and blend for ten seconds. Fold in nuts and marshmallows. Batter will be lumpy. Spoon into greased muffin cups until three-fourths full. Bake until tester comes out clean.

Bake at 400 degrees 18 to 20 minutes • Makes 16 muffins.

• Blend dry ingredients together in one bowl, liquid ingredients in another. Then add liquid ingredients into a well made in the center of the dry ingredients, stirring quickly, 10 to 20 seconds at the most. Don't worry if the batter is lumpy. The less you beat the muffin batter, the lighter your muffins will be.

Mexican Mocha Muffins

Mexicans love dark chocolate and their mole sauce is legendary. These mocha muffins, a masterful blending of coffee, chocolate, pecans and Mexican Kahlua liqueur, are perfect with after-dinner coffee.

1 cup boiling WATER
2 Tbsp. INSTANT COFFEE
3 Tbsp. unsweetened
   CHOCOLATE COCOA MIX
2 Tbsp. VANILLA
½ cup KAHLUA
2⅔ cups FLOUR
1½ tsp. BAKING POWDER

1 tsp. SODA
½ tsp. SALT
1 cup SUGAR
1 cup chopped PECANS
2 EGGS
3 tsp. BUTTER, melted
¾ cup BUTTERMILK

Boil water and add to instant coffee and cocoa to make one cup, stirring well. Add vanilla and Kahlua to the coffee mixture. Set aside.

Sift together flour, baking powder, soda, salt and sugar in large bowl. Stir in pecans. In small bowl, whisk eggs, melted butter and buttermilk. Stir in coffee mixture, blending well. Make a well in the dry ingredients and add the liquid, stirring quickly and lightly. Spoon batter into greased muffin cups and bake until done.

Bake at 400 degrees 20 to 25 minutes • Makes 18-20 muffins.

New England Toll House Muffins

If you like Toll House cookies, you'll love these muffins!

2 cups all-purpose FLOUR
2/3 cup BROWN SUGAR
1/3 cup white SUGAR
½ tsp. SALT
2 tsp. BAKING POWDER
1 tsp. SODA
1 EGG

½ cup MILK
1 cup SOUR CREAM
½ cup BUTTER, melted
1 tsp. VANILLA
1 cup chopped WALNUTS
1 cup semi-sweet
   CHOCOLATE MORSELS

Mix all the dry ingredients in a large bowl. In another bowl, whisk egg, milk, sour cream, melted butter and vanilla. Make a well in the dry ingredients and add wet ingredients, blending lightly. Quickly fold in nuts and chocolate morsels. Spoon into greased muffin tins and bake until tester comes out clean.

Bake at 375 degrees 20 minutes • Makes 18 muffins.

Peppermint Patty Muffins

Peppermint has been used as a carminative, a cure for indigestion and digestive aid in England since the early sixteenth century. This usage still prevails in our modern custom of serving after dinner mints. Try these Peppermint Patty Muffins for a delicious conclusion to your meals.

1½ cups FLOUR
¼ cup SUGAR
4 Tbsp. COCOA or
   chocolate powder
2 Tbsp. BAKING POWDER
½ tsp. SALT

1 EGG
¾ cup MILK
¼ cup melted BUTTER
¼ tsp. PEPPERMINT EXTRACT
12 CHOCOLATE MINT
   PATTIES

Combine the first five ingredients in a large bowl and stir well to blend. Whisk the next four ingredients in a small bowl. Pour the wet ingredients into a well in the center of the dry ingredients. Stir 10 seconds and spoon enough batter into each greased muffin pan to fill half full. Then place one chocolate covered round peppermint patty in the center of each muffin and cover completely with remaining batter. Bake the full 20 minutes and cool for five minutes to allow the peppermint center to congeal.

Bake at 375 degrees 20 minutes • Makes 12 muffins.

• Grease your muffin tins in advance, so that you can pop the muffins right into the oven after mixing. The new lecithin cooking sprays make the job quick and easy.

New York Chocolate Cheesecake Muffins

New Yorkers say their cheesecake is the best in the world. These muffins combine a rich cheesecake center with dark chocolate cake— irresistible!

3 oz. CREAM CHEESE
2 Tbsp. SUGAR
½ cup chopped WALNUTS
1 cup FLOUR
¼ cup SUGAR
5 Tbsp. sweetened
   CHOCOLATE COCOA MIX

2 tsp. BAKING POWDER
½ tsp. SALT
1 EGG, beaten
¾ cup MILK
1/3 cup OIL

In a small bowl, blend cream cheese and sugar till fluffy. Add chopped walnuts and set aside. In a large bowl combine flour, sugar, cocoa, baking powder and salt. Combine egg, milk and oil in another bowl. Make a well in the center of the dry ingredients and add milk mixture. Batter will be thin and lumpy.

Spoon about one tablespoon chocolate batter into each greased muffin cup. Drop one teaspoon of the cream cheese mixture on top and then more chocolate batter. Bake immediately.

Bake at 375 degrees 18 to 20 minutes • Makes 12 muffins.

• Blend dry ingredients together in one bowl, liquid ingredients in another. Then add liquid ingredients into a well made in the center of the dry ingredients, stirring quickly, 10 to 20 seconds at the most. Don't worry if the batter is lumpy. The less you beat the muffin batter, the lighter your muffins will be.

*A miscellany
of dessert muffins...*

Ohio
Cherry Cobbler Muffins

A blue ribbon cherry cobbler from a recent Ohio State Fair inspired these delectable dessert muffins. Serve them warm with vanilla ice cream for a special treat.

1 can CHERRY PIE FILLING
1 tsp. LEMON JUICE
½ tsp. ALMOND EXTRACT
1½ cups FLOUR
1/3 cup SUGAR
1½ tsp. BAKING POWDER
½ tsp. SODA
¼ tsp. SALT
½ tsp. CINNAMON
½ cup chopped PECANS
1 EGG
2 Tbsp. BUTTER, melted
1¼ cups BUTTERMILK
CINNAMON SUGAR

Separate one cup cherries from pie filling. Add lemon juice and almond extract. Set aside. Mix together flour, sugar, baking powder, soda, salt and cinnamon. Blend in pecans. In another bowl, whisk egg with melted butter and buttermilk. Add to dry ingredients, mixing together lightly. Fill muffin cups one-half full. Drop two cherries into each muffin cup, then cover with batter. Sprinkle tops with cinnamon sugar and bake until lightly browned.

Bake at 400 degrees 20-22 minutes • Makes 12 muffins.

Peach Melba Muffins

The French dessert Peach Melba, created by the great chef Escoffier for opera star Nellie Melba, inspired this delicious dessert muffin. Serve warm Peach Melba Muffins with ice cream for a modern version of the classic French dessert. C'est magnifique!

1 cup PEACHES, diced
  (and drained, if canned)
½ tsp. CINNAMON
2 cups all-purpose FLOUR
½ cup SUGAR
2½ tsp. BAKING POWDER
½ tsp. SALT

½ cup chopped WALNUTS
1 EGG, lightly-beaten
1 cup MILK
1/3 cup BUTTER or
  margarine, melted
2 Tbsp. BRANDY
1 jar RASPBERRY JAM

Dice 1 cup drained peaches and sprinkle with one-half teaspoon cinnamon. Set aside.

Sift together flour, sugar, baking powder and salt. Stir in chopped walnuts. Whisk together egg, milk, melted butter and brandy. Stir peaches and cinnamon together with egg mixture. Make a well in the dry ingredients and add the moist ingredients, mixing lightly and quickly. Fill greased muffin cups one-half full. Add one spoonful of raspberry jam, covering lightly with batter until tins are two-thirds full. Bake until golden brown and tester comes out clean.

Bake at 400 degrees 20-25 minutes • Makes 12 muffins.

Italian Amaretto Muffins

Combining almonds with the subtle taste of Amaretto, this is a delicious muffin for dessert or tea, especially good with fresh fruit.

2 cups all-purpose FLOUR
½ cup SUGAR
1½ tsp. BAKING POWDER
½ tsp. BAKING SODA
¼ tsp. SALT

1 cup chopped ALMONDS
1 EGG, beaten
1 cup BUTTERMILK
1/3 cup BUTTER, melted
½ cup AMARETTO

Mix together flour, sugar, baking powder, soda and salt. Stir in chopped almonds. In another bowl, whisk egg, buttermilk, melted butter, and Amaretto. Make a well in the dry ingredients and add liquid ingredients, mixing quickly. Spoon into greased muffin pans and bake until lightly brown and tester comes out clean.

Bake at 400 degrees 15-20 minutes • Makes 14 muffins.

French Brandied Cherry Muffins

The French are famous for their fabulous desserts made with fruits and brandy. Try French Brandied Cherry Muffins when you're in a luxurious mood.

2 cups (16-oz. can)
  SOUR CHERRIES
½ cup BRANDY
2 cups FLOUR
¾ cup SUGAR
1½ tsp. BAKING POWDER

½ tsp. SODA
pinch SALT
¾ cup BUTTER
1 EGG
1 cup SOUR CREAM
2 Tbsp. reserved BRANDY

Drain two cups sour cherries and soak overnight in one-half cup brandy. Drain well before tossing in with dry ingredients. Reserve brandy for later.

Mix dry ingredients in a large bowl. Cut in butter as you would when making a pie crust. Whisk egg, sour cream and two tablespoons brandy. Stir into dry ingredients, mixing quickly. Fold in cherries. Batter will be lumpy. Fill muffin pans three-fourths full and bake until tester comes out clean.

Bake at 375 degrees 20 minutes • Makes 16 muffins.

Spanish Coconut Muffins

Inspired by the luscious coconut pudding served in Spain, these Spanish Coconut Muffins are pudding-rich. Serve with fresh fruit and coffee for a special dessert. Muy bueno!

1½ cups FLOUR
1½ tsp. BAKING POWDER
½ tsp. SODA
½ cup SUGAR
1 cup grated COCONUT
1 tsp. grated ORANGE RIND

2 EGGS
4 Tbsp. BUTTER, melted
1 tsp. VANILLA
¼ cup WHITE WINE
2/3 cup BUTTERMILK
chopped ALMONDS

Sift together flour, baking powder, soda and sugar. Add coconut and grated orange rind. In another bowl, whisk eggs with melted butter, vanilla, white wine and buttermilk. Quickly combine with dry ingredients, blending lightly. Spoon into greased muffin tins and top with chopped almonds. Bake until golden.

Bake at 400 degrees 15-20 minutes • Makes 12-14 muffins.

Hawaiian Pineapple Muffins

Hawaiian Pineapple Muffins offer a taste of paradise—great with desserts, tea or Polynesian food.

1 EGG
1 cup unsweetened
   PINEAPPLE JUICE
¼ cup melted SHORTENING
2 cups FLOUR
½ tsp. SALT

4 tsp. BAKING POWDER
¼ cup SUGAR
½ cup well-drained
   crushed PINEAPPLE
2 Tbsp. SUGAR
1 tsp. grated ORANGE RIND

Beat egg and pineapple juice. Add shortening. Add flour sifted with salt, baking powder and sugar. Stir just until moistened. Fold in drained pineapple. Fill greased muffin tins two-thirds full and sprinkle with two tablespoons sugar and grated orange rind. Bake until done.

Bake at 400 degrees 25 minutes • Makes 12 muffins.

Haifa Honey-Orange Muffins

From Israel, the land of milk and honey and sweet Haifa oranges, comes the inspiration for these delectable muffins. Serve with fresh fruit for a light dessert. Also delicious for breakfast or tea.

2½ cups FLOUR
1/3 cup WHEAT GERM
¼ cup SUGAR
1 Tbsp. grated ORANGE PEEL
2½ tsp. BAKING POWDER
1½ tsp. BAKING SODA

1¼ tsp. SALT
¾ cup BUTTER or margarine
   melted and cooled
½ cup HONEY
¼ cup ORANGE JUICE
3 EGGS

In a large bowl, combine flour, wheat germ, sugar, orange peel, baking powder, soda and salt. In a small bowl, combine remaining ingredients. Add this to dry ingredients, blending quickly. Fill greased muffin cups two-thirds full with batter. Bake for 15 to 20 minutes or until toothpick comes out clean when inserted into center.

Bake at 375 degrees 15 to 20 minutes • Makes 24 muffins.

Piña Colada Muffins

Pina Colada Muffins have captured the taste of the tropics. Try them for dessert with fresh sliced pineapple, strawberries and papayas for a mini-vacation.

1¾ cups all-purpose FLOUR
½ tsp. SALT
¼ cup SUGAR
2 tsp. BAKING POWDER
2 EGGS
2 tsp. RUM FLAVORING
3 Tbsp. melted BUTTER
¼ cup MILK

¾ cup CREAM OF COCONUT
(available at liquor stores—
open and stir *thoroughly*
before using)
¾ cup shredded COCONUT
¾ cup crushed PINEAPPLE,
drained

Sift the dry ingredients together in a large bowl. In a smaller bowl, beat the eggs, then add rum flavoring, melted butter, milk and cream of coconut. Mix thoroughly. Blend shredded coconut into the egg-milk mixture. Make a well in the dry ingredients and mix in the wet ingredients, blending lightly. Fold in the crushed pineapple. Spoon into greased muffin cups and bake until golden brown.

Bake at 400 degrees 20 to 25 minutes • Makes 15 muffins.

Chinese Almond Muffins

Serve Chinese Almond Muffins with orange sherbet or mandarin oranges sprinkled with shredded coconut after a Chinese dinner. Also good with tea.

1⅓ cups all-purpose FLOUR
½ cup SUGAR
1 Tbsp. BAKING POWDER
2/3 cup sliced ALMONDS
1 EGG

1 cup MILK
2½ tsp. ALMOND EXTRACT
¼ cup BUTTER, melted
12 whole ALMONDS,
for garnish

Whisk together all the dry ingredients. Stir in almonds. In another bowl, whisk eggs, milk, almond extract and melted butter. Make a well in the dry ingredients and add liquid ingredients, mixing quickly. Batter will be lumpy. Spoon into greased muffin cups three-fourths full. Top each muffin with one whole almond. Bake until brown and tester comes out clean.

Bake at 375 degrees 20-25 minutes • Makes 12 muffins.

Graham Cracker Muffins

Did you know that graham crackers were originally a health food? They were named for Sylvester Graham, a nineteenth-century American reformer who advocated a vegetable diet and coarsely-ground whole wheat flour as a cure for intemperance. Children love graham crackers and will enjoy these muffins for desserts or after school snacks.

32 GRAHAM CRACKERS, crumbled
4 Tbsp. SUGAR
½ tsp. SALT
4 Tbsp. melted BUTTER or margarine

1 cup scalded MILK
2 EGGS, beaten
4 tsp. BAKING POWDER
1 cup RAISINS
1 cup ALMONDS, chopped coarsely

Crumble crackers. Add sugar, salt and butter. Pour hot milk over and beat well. Add remaining ingredients and spoon mixture into muffin pans, filling two-thirds full. Bake until golden and tester comes out clean.

Bake at 400 to 425 degrees 20 minutes • Makes 12 muffins.

Irish Coffee Muffins

A fanciful after dinner treat, Irish Coffee Muffins offer a subtle mixture of coffee, cream and a touch of Irish whiskey. Irish coffee muffins are especially delicious served warm and topped with vanilla ice cream.

1 cup strong COFFEE (instant, regular or decaffeinated)
2½ cups all-purpose FLOUR
1½ tsp. BAKING POWDER
1 tsp. SODA

½ tsp. SALT
1 cup SUGAR
2 EGGS
1 cup SOUR CREAM
4 Tbsp. IRISH WHISKEY

Brew one cup strong coffee (instant, regular or decaffeinated). Set aside.

Mix together flour, baking powder, soda, salt and sugar. In another bowl whisk eggs with sour cream. Add coffee and Irish whiskey. Make a well in the dry ingredients and add all the liquid ingredients, blending lightly and quickly. Spoon batter into greased muffin tins and bake 20 minutes or until done.

Bake at 400 degrees 20 to 25 minutes • Makes 18 muffins.

Pineapple Upside Down Muffins

For a new angle on dessert muffins, try these Pineapple Upside Down Muffins, inspired by Mary Ann Dreher's recipe for pineapple upside down cake, a favorite dessert in the American south.

¼ cup BUTTER, melted
1/3 cup BROWN SUGAR
1 cup (8-oz) crushed PINEAPPLE
   (drained)
1½ cups all-purpose FLOUR
½ cup SUGAR
¼ tsp. SALT

½ tsp. SODA
1 tsp. BAKING POWDER
1 tsp. CINNAMON
2 EGGS, beaten
1 cup BUTTERMILK
2 Tbsp. BUTTER, melted

Grease muffin cups. Spoon one-fourth cup melted butter evenly into 12 muffin cups. Sprinkle brown sugar over butter, then arrange pineapple in butter-sugar mixture. Set aside.

Mix together all the dry ingredients (flour, sugar, salt, soda, baking powder and cinnamon) in large bowl. In another bowl, whisk eggs with buttermilk and two tablespoons melted butter. Make a well in the dry ingredients and quickly blend in the wet ingredients. Spoon into muffin cups on top of the pineapple mixture. Bake until done and gently remove from pans when cool, setting muffins upside down on tray and replacing any pineapple chunks which may have stuck to bottom of pan. Serve warm.

Bake at 375 degrees 20-25 minutes • Makes 12 muffins.

• Remember to mix dry ingredients together well, in order to distribute the baking powder and baking soda evenly.

Greek Baklava Muffins

These delicious Greek Baklava Muffins are filled with chopped walnuts, butter and cinnamon, then drizzled with honey. A sweet treat after meals or for a festive tea.

Filling:

1 cup chopped WALNUTS	1½ tsp. CINNAMON
1/3 cup SUGAR	3 Tbsp. BUTTER, melted
2 Tbsp. BROWN SUGAR	

Mix filling ingredients together in a small bowl. Set aside.

1½ cups FLOUR	1 EGG
2 tsp. BAKING POWDER	3 Tbsp. BUTTER, melted
½ tsp. SODA	1 cup BUTTERMILK
½ cup SUGAR	

Topping: ½ cup HONEY

Combine flour, baking powder, soda and sugar in a large bowl. In another bowl, whisk egg, melted butter and buttermilk. Add to dry ingredients, stirring quickly until mixed. Fill greased muffin cups one-third full, add one tablespoon filling, then cover with batter until two-thirds full. Sprinkle any remaining filling on top. Bake until golden brown. Remove from muffin tins and drizzle with honey.

Bake at 400 degrees 15-20 minutes • Makes 12-14 muffins.

• Always preheat oven. Never put muffins into a cold oven.

Appalachian Bread Pudding Muffins

Bread pudding is a traditional dessert in Appalachia and a clever way of using leftover biscuits. These Appalachian Bread Pudding Muffins are delicious for dessert or teatime.

1 cup coarse BREAD CUBES
1 cup BUTTERMILK
1½ cups FLOUR
½ cup BROWN SUGAR
3 tsp. BAKING POWDER
1 tsp. SODA
2/3 cup RAISINS

½ cup grated COCONUT
½ cup chopped NUTS
2 EGGS
4 Tbsp. BUTTER, melted
1 tsp. VANILLA
NUTMEG

Soak bread cubes in one cup buttermilk. Set aside. In a large bowl, sift together flour, brown sugar, baking powder and soda. Stir in raisins, coconut and chopped nuts. Whisk eggs with butter and vanilla and add to buttermilk mixture. Make a well in dry ingredients and add wet ingredients, stirring 10 seconds. Fill greased muffin tins nearly full. Sprinkle tops with nutmeg and bake until done.

Bake at 375 degrees 20-22 minutes • Makes 12 muffins.

Washington Cherry Nut Muffins

Cherries have a long association with America's first president, George Washington, who supposedly cut down a cherry tree and could not tell a lie. Thousands of cherry blossoms bloom each spring in our nation's capital, Washington, D.C. These pink Washington Cherry Nut Muffins are a special treat for dessert or tea.

2 cups FLOUR
4 tsp. BAKING POWDER
½ cup chopped ALMONDS
½ cup WHEAT GERM
1 tsp. SALT
2 Tbsp. coarsely-grated
  ORANGE RIND

2 EGGS
¼ cup dark BROWN SUGAR
1 tsp. ALMOND EXTRACT
¼ cup SAFFLOWER OIL
1 (21-oz.) can CHERRY
  PIE FILLING

Combine first six ingredients in large mixing bowl and mix thoroughly. Whisk eggs, sugar, almond extract and oil until well blended. Add cherries, juice and all. Presweetened pie cherries cut down on the sugar needed. Blend together quickly and spoon into muffin tins. Bake until they just begin to brown on top.

Bake at 375 degrees 22 to 25 minutes • Makes 15 muffins.

Minnesota
Sour Cream Muffins

The happiest memories of Gen Farrow's childhood centered around her grandfather's apple orchards, vegetable gardens and the wonderful sour cream that came with the hot summers before electricity was introduced in rural Minnesota. These Minnesota Sour Cream Muffins combine the produce of the farms with the hazelnuts found in the nearby woods.

1½ cups grated APPLES
  (leave skins on)
1 cup peeled, grated CARROTS
½ cup toasted HAZELNUTS
1¼ cups SOUR CREAM
1 cup DARK BROWN SUGAR
2 EGGS

2 tsp. VANILLA
1 tsp. SALT
2¼ cups all-purpose
  unbleached FLOUR
1 tsp. SODA
1 Tbsp. BAKING POWDER
½ cup BRAN

Mix apples, carrots and nuts together. Whisk sour cream, sugar, eggs, vanilla and salt together well in another bowl. Stir together flour, soda, baking powder and bran in a separate bowl. Pour the sour cream sugar mixture over the grated carrots, nuts and apples. Stir until blended. Add the flour mixture and stir quickly, not over 10 seconds. Spoon into greased muffin tins and bake until golden. Serve warm.

Bake at 375 degrees 20-25 minutes • Makes 22 muffins.

• Grease your muffin tins in advance, so that you can pop the muffins right into the oven after mixing. The new lecithin cooking sprays make the job quick and easy.

Hazelnut Autumn Muffins

Hazelnuts come shelled, but the brown outside "skin" or husk is much like a peanut skin. In this recipe we remove some of the skin.

3 cups FLOUR
1 cup toasted HAZELNUTS
1 Tbsp. BAKING POWDER
1 tsp. SODA
2/3 cup SUGAR
¾ cup FRANGELICO LIQUEUR

3 EGGS
1 cup BUTTERMILK
½ cup MILK
¾ cup BUTTER or
    margarine, melted
SALT, if desired

Toast the cupful of hazelnuts in the oven and then pour into a clean towel. Cover and rub with a light touch so some of the brown husk will be removed. Then grind the hazelnuts to a flour-like meal.

Place first five ingredients in large bowl. Combine the next six and whisk well until blended. Pour liquid into dry ingredients and stir quickly before spooning into greased pans. Place in preheated oven.

Bake at 400 degrees 18 to 20 minutes • Makes 26 muffins.

Italian Hazelnut Muffins

The Italians have made a delicate hazelnut liqueur for centuries. We combined the liqueur with toasted hazelnuts to create these distinctive dessert muffins. Serve warm with ice cream as a light dessert after your next Italian meal.

1½ cups unbleached FLOUR
1 cup toasted, chopped
    HAZELNUTS
2 tsp. BAKING POWDER
1 tsp. SODA
1 tsp. SALT

2 EGGS
2/3 cup BROWN SUGAR
2/3 cup FRANGELICO
    HAZELNUT LIQUEUR
6 Tbsp. melted BUTTER
    or margarine

Combine the first five ingredients in a large mixing bowl. Whisk the eggs, sugar, liqueur and shortening together until well blended. Add quickly to dry ingredients, stirring not more than 10 seconds. Spoon batter into sprayed muffin pans and bake until done.

Bake at 375 degrees 18 to 20 minutes • Makes 12 muffins.

Gingerbread Muffins

Almost every European country has its own traditional gingerbread, dating back to the Middle Ages. In the Renaissance, lavishly decorated gingerbread men were a Christmas favorite of Queen Elizabeth I. Gingerbread was also believed to comfort the stomach and liven the spirits. We added chopped walnuts to our gingerbread for extra appeal and serve these dark, spicy muffins topped with freshly whipped cream.

1 beaten EGG
½ cup SUGAR
½ cup light MOLASSES
¼ cup SALAD OIL
1 cup FLOUR
¼ tsp. SALT
½ tsp. SODA

½ tsp. GINGER
¼ tsp. NUTMEG
¼ tsp. CINNAMON
½ cup boiling WATER
½ cup chopped WALNUTS
(optional)

Combine egg, sugar, molasses and oil. Beat well. In another bowl, mix flour, salt, soda and spices. Combine with egg mixture, then add water. Fold in nuts if desired. Fill greased muffin tins two-thirds full and bake until done.

Bake at 350 degrees 20 minutes • Makes 12 muffins.

• To store muffins, simply freeze them in tightly-closed plastic bags after letting them cool. Muffins keep in the freezer up to three months. Just thaw them out when ready to use.

Southern Pumpkin Pecan Muffins

Pumpkin, molasses, brown sugar, Georgia pecans and fragrant spices combine to produce the delicate flavor of this dessert muffin from the old South. Serve warm with cream cheese or ice cream.

2¾ cups unbleached FLOUR	1 cup chopped PECANS
1 Tbsp. BAKING POWDER	2 EGGS
1 tsp. SODA	2 cups PUMPKIN PUREE
1 tsp. CINNAMON	1 cup SOUR CREAM
1 tsp. NUTMEG	¼ cup light MOLASSES
1 tsp. GINGER	¾ cup BROWN SUGAR

Combine the first seven ingredients and mix well. In a smaller bowl, whisk the eggs, pumpkin, sour cream, molasses and sugar until sugar is dissolved. Pour liquid ingredients into center of dry ingredients. Stir quickly until flour disappears and spoon into greased muffin tins. Bake until lightly brown.

Bake at 375 degrees 25 minutes • Makes 22 muffins.

Curaçao Orange Muffins

Many years ago on the Dutch Island of Curacao in the picturesque Caribbean, two brothers began to raise oranges on a farm a few miles outside the city of Willemstad. But the oranges, though beautiful to look at, were so bitter they were inedible. Undaunted, the brothers boiled the bitter oranges with sugar and distilled a liqueur which they named Curacao. Enjoy these delicious Curacao Orange Muffins warm for dessert or tea.

3 cups FLOUR	½ cup CURAÇAO
3 tsp. BAKING POWDER	3 beaten EGGS
1 tsp. SODA	1 tsp. VANILLA
¾ cup BUTTER, melted	grated RIND from
1¼ cups SUGAR	2 large ORANGES
½ cup ORANGE JUICE	

Mix flour, baking powder and soda in a large bowl. Melt butter and pour over sugar in another bowl. Stir until sugar is dissolved. Add orange juice, Curacao, eggs, vanilla and grated orange rind. Blend Curacao egg mixture with the dry ingredients, stirring quickly. Fill muffin tins two-thirds full and bake until done.

Bake at 350 degrees 22 minutes • Makes 23 muffins.

Old English Mincemeat Muffins

Rich, spicy mincemeat pie was a Yuletide favorite in Merry Old England. Disapproving Puritans called it "superstitious pie," but it was still delicious. Serve up a modern variation—Old English Mincemeat Muffins, chock full of raisins, currants, cinnamon and spices.

1 cup unbleached FLOUR
½ cup whole wheat
   pastry FLOUR
1½ tsp. BAKING POWDER
½ tsp. SODA
½ cup SUGAR

1½ tsp. CINNAMON
2 EGGS, beaten
3 Tbsp. BUTTER, melted
1 cup BUTTERMILK
1 cup MINCEMEAT (use prepared
   mincemeat for convenience)

Mix together white and whole wheat flour, baking powder, soda, sugar and cinnamon in a large bowl. In another bowl, whisk eggs with melted butter and buttermilk. Make a well in dry ingredients and quickly stir in liquid ingredients.

Cover bottoms of greased muffin cups with one spoonful of batter each. Spoon in one heaping tablespoon of mincemeat. Cover with remaining batter. Bake until golden brown—your kitchen will be filled with spicy fragrance. Serve warm.

Bake at 400 degrees 15-20 minutes • Makes 12 muffins.

Georgia Peach Muffins

Peachtree Street in downtown Atlanta, is named after Georgia's delicious peaches. These Georgia Peach Muffins combine peaches with pecans, another Georgia specialty, for a memorable dessert or teatime favorite.

Topping:
- 3 Tbsp. FLOUR
- 1 Tbsp. BROWN SUGAR
- ½ tsp. CINNAMON
- 1 Tbsp. melted BUTTER

In a small bowl, stir all ingredients together with a fork. Blend in one tablespoon melted butter. Set aside for topping.

- 1½ cups chopped, canned PEACHES, drained
- 1 tsp. CINNAMON
- 1 cup unbleached FLOUR
- ½ cup whole wheat pastry FLOUR
- 1/3 cup SUGAR
- 1½ tsp. BAKING POWDER
- ½ tsp. SODA
- ¼ tsp. SALT
- ½ cup chopped PECANS
- 1 EGG
- 2 Tbsp. melted BUTTER
- 1 cup BUTTERMILK

Sprinkle peaches with cinnamon. Set aside. In a large bowl, sift together flour, whole wheat flour, sugar, baking powder, soda, salt and pecans. In another bowl, whisk egg, melted butter and buttermilk. Add quickly to dry ingredients. Fold in sliced peaches. Spoon batter into greased muffin tins and sprinkle on topping. Bake until done and serve warm.

Bake at 400 degrees 15-20 minutes • Makes 15 muffins.

Middle East Apricot Almond Muffins

Apricots were grown in the famous hanging gardens of Babylon and are still raised in Iraq and Turkey. They have been used in cordials and homeopathic cures for centuries. With their high vitamin A content, which stimulates the immune system, they are considered a valuable health food today. These apricot muffins are a delicious ounce of prevention for dessert or tea.

1 cup APRICOT PUREE
  (see directions below)*
1 cup BUTTERMILK
¼ cup SAFFLOWER OIL
½ cup dark BROWN SUGAR
2 EGGS
1 tsp. ALMOND EXTRACT

1¾ cups unbleached FLOUR
1 cup diced, dried APRICOTS
1 Tbsp. BAKING POWDER
1 tsp. SODA
1 tsp. SALT
½ cup ground ALMONDS

Whisk together the first six ingredients. Combine the remaining six ingredients well, being sure the diced apricots are separated and covered with flour. Make a well and pour the liquid in, stirring quickly. Spoon into prepared muffin pans, filling almost full. Bake until lightly brown on top.

Bake at 400 degrees 18 to 20 minutes • Makes 20 muffins.

*For apricot puree: Begin with one pound dried apricots. Dice one cupful to go into the batter uncooked in their natural dried state. This increases the apricot taste in the muffin. Cover the remaining apricots with water and let soak overnight. In the morning, drain off the water, add fresh water but do not cover. Bring to the simmering stage and let simmer for about 10 minutes. Let stand until cool. Puree in food processor.

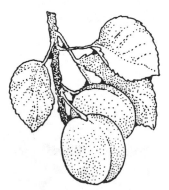

Danish Coffee Cream Puff Muffins

Danish desserts make ample use of cream, sour cream and butter from Denmark's thriving dairies. A walk through Copenhagen's Tivoli Gardens is hardly complete without sampling the luxurious creamy Danish desserts which inspired this light sour cream muffin with the mocha cream filling. Try it with dark Scandinavian coffee for a special dessert treat.

5 oz. CREAM CHEESE, room temperature	2 tsp. BAKING POWDER
1 Tbsp. INSTANT COFFEE	1 tsp. SODA
1 Tbsp. POWDERED SUGAR	½ tsp. SALT
1 tsp. ground CHOCOLATE or cocoa	2 EGGS
1¾ cups unbleached FLOUR	1 cup SOUR CREAM
	½ cup SUGAR
	1 tsp. VANILLA

In a small bowl mix together the cream cheese, instant coffee, powdered sugar and chocolate. Set aside. In a large bowl, mix the flour, baking powder, soda and salt. In another bowl, whisk eggs with sour cream, sugar and vanilla. Make a well in the center of the dry ingredients and pour in the egg, sour cream mixture, stirring for 10 seconds. Dough will be quite thick. Spoon batter into greased muffin pans to about one-third full. Then drop a heaping teaspoonful of the cream cheese mixture into the center of each muffin, being sure it doesn't touch the edges of the pan. Top with the remaining batter, making sure it covers the filling. Place into preheated oven on center rack and bake until done.

Bake at 375 degrees 18 to 20 minutes • Makes 12 muffins.

Swedish Shrove Tuesday Muffins

Swedish *semlor*, delicate cardamon buns filled with almond paste and dusted with powdered sugar, are traditionally served on Shrove Tuesday. These Swedish Shrove Tuesday Muffins are delicious any time of the year. Serve with whipped cream or hot vanilla sauce for a final Swedish touch.

5 oz. CREAM CHEESE
7 oz. pkg. MARZIPAN
  (almond paste)
¼ cup ground ALMONDS
1½ cups FLOUR
2 tsp. BAKING POWDER
1 tsp. SODA

1 tsp. SALT
1 tsp. ground CARDAMON
2 EGGS
1 cup SOUR CREAM
½ cup SUGAR
1 tsp. ALMOND EXTRACT
POWDERED SUGAR

Combine cream cheese, marzipan and ground almonds by heating in a small saucepan on low, stirring until melted. Set aside. In a large bowl combine flour, baking powder, soda, salt and cardamon and stir well. Whisk the eggs, sour cream, sugar and almond extract until well blended. Make a well in the dry ingredients, adding the liquid and stirring only 10 seconds. Spoon into greased muffin pans, filling one-third full. Place a teaspoon of the marzipan mixture in the center. Completely cover with more batter. Bake on middle rack until done. Remove from oven. Let cool about five minutes, then remove from muffin pans, and dust with powdered sugar.

Bake at 375 degrees 15 to 18 minutes • Makes 14 muffins.

Microwave Muffins

Nothing can top the taste of homemade muffins, fresh from the oven. But the magic of microwave has added new speed to cooking. Not only can you easily melt butter or margarine for conventional recipes, you can bake a batch of muffins from scratch in less than five minutes.

Unbelievable? Try it for yourself. These easy recipes will get you started. But there are a few things you should know. Breads baked in microwave ovens have a different consistency than those baked conventionally. Because they do not brown, their tops can look pale and unappealing. Our microwave recipes compensate with colorful and crunchy toppings.

Also, you must use special microwave pans or custard cups, *not* metal muffin tins, which can seriously damage your microwave oven. Paper muffin cups are a *must* to keep the muffins from retaining too much moisture during the cooking process.

To keep muffins cooking evenly, stop the oven and rotate the pan every minute during the cooking cycle. This is not too difficult as muffins usually cook in three to four minutes.

Because all microwave ovens function differently, use our cooking times as guides and check for doneness at the lowest time. If muffins aren't done, cook a little longer. But do not overcook, or muffins will be tough.

When muffins are done, tiny bubbles will pop on the surface as they do on the tops of pancakes when they are ready to turn. Muffins may still be slightly moist on top, but when scratched with a toothpick, the dough will be done beneath the surface. Small moist spots will disappear when standing.

After the short baking cycle, microwave muffins should cool on a rack for five minutes before serving to release excess moisture. Using a knife to support their weight, carefully remove muffins from pans and stand them on a rack in their paper liners.

Try these microwave muffins for an unbelievably quick and delicious addition to your meals.

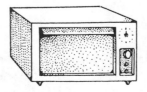

California Bran Microwave Muffins

This microwave muffin batter will keep up to two weeks in the refrigerator. Mix up a batch in advance and bake hot muffins in the morning before your coffee has finished perking.

½ cup WATER
2/3 cup WHOLE BRAN CEREAL
2 Tbsp. BUTTER or margarine
½ cup BUTTERMILK
1 EGG, beaten
2 Tbsp. BROWN SUGAR
2 Tbsp. HONEY
1 Tbsp. MOLASSES

½ cup unbleached FLOUR
1/3 cup whole wheat FLOUR
2 Tbsp. WHEAT GERM
1¼ tsp. BAKING POWDER
¼ tsp. BAKING SODA
½ cup RAISINS
WHEAT GERM or
    sesame seeds

Heat water in microwave on high for one to two minutes or until boiling. Put bran cereal and margarine in bowl and pour boiling water on top. Add buttermilk, egg, brown sugar, honey and molasses. In another bowl, mix flour, whole wheat flour, wheat germ, baking powder and soda. Combine liquid with dry ingredients. Fold in raisins. Spoon into paper-lined microwave muffin pans and top with wheat germ or sesame seeds. Bake on high for 2½ to 4 minutes, stopping oven and turning pan every minute to ensure even baking. Muffins are done when tops are nearly dry and bubbles burst on top. Scratch with a toothpick to see that dough is done beneath the surface. Remove from pans and cool for five minutes on wire rack.

Bake on high 2½ to 4 minutes • Makes 12 muffins.

- Pop frozen muffins into the microwave for one minute or less on "reheat." For conventional ovens, wrap frozen muffins in aluminum foil and heat for 10-15 minutes at 350 degrees.

Irish Jam Microwave Muffins

Try these quick Irish Jam Microwave Muffins for tea or brunch.

¾ cup FLOUR	1/3 cup BUTTERMILK
¾ tsp. BAKING POWDER	3 Tbsp. COOKING OIL
¼ tsp. SODA	¼ tsp. LEMON EXTRACT
½ tsp. grated LEMON RIND	Raspberry or Blueberry JAM
2 Tbsp. SUGAR	CONFECTIONER'S SUGAR
1 EGG	CINNAMON

Mix together flour, baking powder, soda, grated lemon rind and sugar. In another bowl, whisk egg with buttermilk, oil and lemon extract. Quickly combine with dry ingredients, stirring lightly. Place one tablespoon batter into paper-lined microwave muffin pan. Then add one tablespoon jam and cover with batter. Bake on high 2½ to 4 minutes until done. Gently remove from pan and cool on wire rack, dusting tops with confectioner's sugar and cinnamon.

Bake on high 2½ to 4 minutes • Makes 6 muffins.

Iowa Crunch Microwave Muffins

A delightful peanut butter topping makes Iowa Crunch Muffins a snack time favorite. This microwave version is really speedy.

Topping:

1½ Tbsp. PEANUT BUTTER	1 Tbsp. FLOUR
2 Tbsp. SUGAR	pinch SALT

Mix together topping ingredients well with a fork. Set aside.

¾ cup FLOUR	1 EGG
¾ tsp. BAKING POWDER	1/3 cup BUTTERMILK
¼ tsp. SODA	3 Tbsp. COOKING OIL
2 Tbsp. SUGAR	

Combine flour, baking powder, soda and sugar. In another bowl, whisk egg with buttermilk and oil. Combine with dry ingredients, stirring lightly and quickly. Spoon into paper-lined microwave muffin cups. Sprinkle on topping. Bake on high for 2½ to 4 minutes until done, stopping oven and rotating pan every minute. Gently remove muffins from pan and cool on wire rack for five minutes.

Bake on high 2½ to 4 minutes • Makes 6 muffins.

Danish Applesauce Microwave Muffins

A crunchy streusel topping makes these muffins especially appealing. Try them for breakfast or tea.

Topping:

2 Tbsp. FLOUR	¼ tsp. CINNAMON
1 Tbsp. BROWN SUGAR	1 Tbsp. melted BUTTER or margarine

Mix together topping ingredients and set aside.

¾ cup FLOUR	¼ cup chopped WALNUTS
¾ tsp. BAKING POWDER	(optional)
¼ tsp. SODA	1 EGG
½ tsp. CINNAMON	1/3 cup APPLESAUCE
¼ tsp. ground CLOVES	⅛ cup BUTTERMILK
	3 Tbsp. COOKING OIL

Mix flour, baking powder, soda, cinnamon and cloves. Add chopped nuts if desired. In another bowl, whisk egg with applesauce, buttermilk and cooking oil. Combine dry and liquid ingredients, mixing lightly and quickly. Spoon batter into six microwave muffin cups with paper liners. Top each muffin with one teaspoon brown sugar mixture. Bake on high 2½ to 4 minutes until done, stopping oven and rotating pan every minute. Remove from pans and cool on wire rack five minutes before serving.

Bake on high 2½ to 4 minutes • Makes 6 muffins.

• Assemble all ingredients in advance to cut down on mixing time.

Southern Corn Fritter Microwave Muffins

Try these light, speedy muffins with bean soup or salad for complementary protein.

¾ cup FLOUR
2 Tbsp. SUGAR
¾ tsp. BAKING POWDER
¼ tsp. SODA
⅛ tsp. BUTTER FLAVORED
   SALT

1 EGG
1/3 cup BUTTERMILK
3 Tbsp. COOKING OIL
2/3 cup canned CORN, drained
BREADCRUMBS
PAPRIKA

Mix together flour, sugar, baking powder, salt and soda in large bowl. In another bowl, whisk egg, buttermilk and oil. Quickly add to dry ingredients. Fold in corn. Spoon batter into paper-lined microwave muffin pan, filling two-thirds full. Top with breadcrumbs and sprinkle with paprika. Bake on high for 2½ to 4 minutes, stopping oven and rotating pan every minute until done. Gently remove muffins from pan and cool for five minutes on wire rack.

Bake on high 2½ to 4 minutes • Makes 6 muffins.

• Be sure your herbs and spices are fresh. All spices lose their potency after a while, and tired spices produce tired tasting muffins.

Ohio Cherry Cobbler Microwave Muffins

Cherries, cinnamon and ground pecans spice up these muffins.

¾ cup FLOUR
2 Tbsp. SUGAR
½ tsp. CINNAMON
¾ tsp. BAKING POWDER
¼ tsp. SODA
2 tsp. ground PECANS

1 EGG
1/3 cup BUTTERMILK
3 Tbsp. COOKING OIL
CHERRY PIE FILLING
4 Tbsp. ground PECANS
CINNAMON SUGAR

Mix flour, sugar, cinnamon, baking powder, soda and two tablespoons ground pecans. In another bowl, whisk egg, buttermilk and cooking oil. Combine with dry ingredients, stirring lightly and quickly. Put one tablespoon of batter in paper-lined microwave muffin cups. Spoon in two cherries from cherry pie filling. Cover with remaining batter. Sprinkle tops with ground pecans and cinnamon sugar. Bake on high for 2½ to 4 minutes until done, stopping oven and rotating pan every minute. When done, gently remove muffins from pan and cool for five minutes on wire rack.

Bake on high 2½ to 4 minutes • Makes 6 muffins.

Hawaiian Pineapple Microwave Muffins

These muffins combine a moist pineapple filling with a crunchy almond topping.

Topping:

4 Tbsp. sliced ALMONDS   1 Tbsp. BROWN SUGAR
1½ Tbsp. melted BUTTER

Combine melted butter with brown sugar and almonds. Set aside.

¾ cup FLOUR   1/3 cup BUTTERMILK
2 Tbsp. SUGAR   3 Tbsp. COOKING OIL
¾ tsp. BAKING POWDER   1 (8-oz.) can crushed
¼ tsp. SODA   PINEAPPLE, drained
1 EGG

Mix flour, sugar, baking powder and soda together in a large bowl. In another bowl, whisk egg with buttermilk and oil. Quickly combine with dry ingredients. Put one tablespoon batter into paper-lined microwave muffin cups. Top with one tablespoon crushed pineapple. Cover with batter until muffin cups are two-thirds full. Top with almond sugar mixture. Bake on high for 2½ to 4 minutes, stopping oven to rotate pan every minute. When done, gently remove muffins from pan and cool on wire rack for five minutes.

Bake on high 2½ to 4 minutes • Makes 6 muffins.

Welsh Rarebit Microwave Muffins

Serve Welsh Rarebit Microwave Muffins with soup and salad for a nutritious light meal.

¾ cup FLOUR
¾ tsp. BAKING POWDER
¼ tsp. SODA
½ tsp. DRY MUSTARD
⅛ tsp. SALT
ground BLACK PEPPER to taste
¾ cup grated CHEDDAR
   CHEESE

1 EGG, beaten
1/3 cup BUTTERMILK
¾ tsp. WORCESTERSHIRE
   SAUCE
3 Tbsp. COOKING OIL
Parmesan CHEESE
PAPRIKA

Combine flour, baking powder, soda and spices in large bowl. Stir in grated cheese. Whisk egg, buttermilk, Worcestershire sauce and oil in another bowl. Combine with dry ingredients, stirring quickly and lightly. Spoon into paper-lined microwave muffin pan and sprinkle tops with parmesan cheese and paprika. Bake on high for 2½ to 4 minutes until done, turning off oven and rotating pan every minute. Test by scratching tops with toothpick. Gently remove muffins from pan and cool for five minutes on wire rack. Serve warm.

Bake on high 2½ to 4 minutes • Makes 6 muffins.

Index to Muffin Recipes

Meet the Authors

It's traditional for Scandinavians to bake, and since **Genevieve Farrow's** grandparents emigrated from Stockholm, Sweden, learning to bake was a natural requirement. In Minnesota, where she grew up, Gen learned to bake an assortment of breads, rolls, cakes and cookies. Her grandmother's Swedish Breakfast Muffins are included in this volume.

When Gen moved to California with her husband, Lyle, and their two young children, Bonnie and Chuck, they discovered a wonderful mixture of different cultures and ethnic foods. The Farrows added California barbecues, Mexican food, Italian, French, Oriental and Greek specialties to their list of family favorites.

Over the years Gen and Lyle have traveled all over the world sampling regional and national cuisines, bringing home their favorite recipes.

Diane Dreher grew up as the child of an Air Force colonel, moving throughout the United States to the Far East and Western Europe. Since Diane's parents are both pilots, exploration is a natural part of family life. The Drehers have celebrated holidays together all over the globe. On vacation, they continue to travel—learning more about local languages, foods and customs, so Diane developed a taste for exotic cuisine early in life.

Diane now writes and teaches in northern California.

Hints for Successful Muffin Making

Your muffins will be lighter when you mix them together quickly and lightly, for this produces the best rising effect. The following tips will help you produce successful muffins every time.

- Always preheat oven. Never put muffins into a cold oven.

- Be sure your herbs and spices are fresh. All spices lose their potency after a while, and tired spices produce tired tasting muffins.

- Assemble all ingredients in advance to cut down on mixing time.

- Grease your muffin tins in advance, so that you can pop the muffins right into the oven after mixing. The new lecithin cooking sprays make the job quick and easy.

- Blend dry ingredients together in one bowl, liquid ingredients in another. Then add liquid ingredients into a well made in the center of the dry ingredients, stirring quickly, 10 to 20 seconds at the most. Don't worry if the batter is lumpy. The less you beat the muffin batter, the lighter your muffins will be.

- Remember to mix dry ingredients together well, in order to distribute the baking powder and baking soda evenly.

- If all the muffin tins are not full, pour water into the empty ones. This will not only save the muffin pans, but will add moisture to the oven and enlarge the muffins while baking.

- Most muffins bake at 400 degrees, but adjust recipes to your own oven. If muffins brown too quickly, then turn your oven down to 375 or even 350.

- Muffins bake best in the middle shelf of your oven. On the lowest shelf, the bottoms brown too quickly. On the highest shelf, the tops brown too soon.

- Muffins are done when they come away from the sides of the pan and when a toothpick or knife inserted into the center comes out dry.

- Let muffins stand a minute or two before removing from tins. They come out more easily that way. Often, you can simply turn the pan upside down over a board and the muffins fall right out. Sometimes you may have to help them out by running a knife along the side of each muffin cup.

- To store muffins, simply freeze them in tightly-closed plastic bags after letting them cool. Muffins keep in the freezer up to three months. Just thaw them out when ready to use.

- Pop frozen muffins into the microwave for one minute or less on "reheat." For conventional ovens, wrap frozen muffins in aluminum foil and heat for 10-15 minutes at 350 degrees.

SALSA LOVERS COOK BOOK

More than 180 taste-tempting recipes for salsas that wi make every meal a special event! Salsas for salads, appe tizers, main dishes, and desserts! Put some salsa in you life! By Susan K. Bollin.

5 1/2 x 8 1/2—128 pages . . . $5.9

CHIP & DIP LOVERS COOK BOOI

More than 150 recipes for fun and festive dips. Mak southwestern dips, dips with fruits and vegetables, meat poultry and seafood. Salsa dips and dips for desserts. Includ recipes for making homemade chips. By Susan K. Bollin.

5 1/2 x 8 1/2—112 pages . . . $5.9

QUICK-N-EASY MEXICAN RECIPES

More than 175 favorite Mexican recipes you can prepa in less than thirty minutes. Traditional items such as tacc tostadas and enchiladas. Features easy recipes for salad soups, breads, desserts and drinks. By Susan K. Bollin.

5 1/2 x 8 1/2—128 pages . . . $5.

CHILI-LOVERS' COOK BOOK

Chili cookoff prize-winning recipes and regional favc ites! The best of chili cookery, from mild to fiery, with a without beans. Plus a variety of taste-tempting foods ma with chile peppers. 150,000 copies in print! By Al a Mildred Fischer.

5 1/2 x 8 1/2—128 pages . . . $5.

CITRUS LOVERS COOK BOOK

Tempting recipes for luscious pies, dazzling desser sunshine salads, novelty meat and seafood dishes! Pl tangy thirst-quenchers with oranges, grapefruits, lemor limes, and tangerines. By Al and Mildred Fischer.

5 1/2 x 8 1/2 — 128 Pages . . . $6.

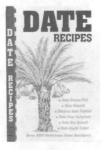

ORDER BLANK

GOLDEN WEST PUBLISHERS

☼ 4113 N. Longview Ave. • Phoenix, AZ 85014

602-265-4392 • **1-800-658-5830** • FAX 602-279-6901

Qty	Title	Price	Amount
	Apple-Lovers' Cook Book	6.95	
	Best Barbecue Recipes	5.95	
	California Favorites Cook Book	5.95	
	Chili-Lovers' Cook Book	5.95	
	Chip and Dip Lovers Cook Book	5.95	
	Christmas in Arizona Cook Book	8.95	
	Christmas in New Mexico Cook Book	8.95	
	Citrus Lovers Cook Book	6.95	
	Cowboy Cartoon Cook Book	5.95	
	Date Recipes	6.95	
	Easy Recipes for Wild Game & Fish	6.95	
	Favorite Pumpkin Recipes	6.95	
	Joy of Muffins	5.95	
	Mexican Desserts & Drinks	6.95	
	Mexican Family Favorites Cook Book	6.95	
	Pecan-Lovers' Cook Book	6.95	
	Quick-n-Easy Mexican Recipes	5.95	
	Recipes for a Healthy Lifestyle	6.95	
	Salsa Lovers Cook Book	5.95	
	Veggie Lovers Cook Book	6.95	
Add $2.00 to total order for shipping & handling			**$2.00**

☐ My Check or Money Order Enclosed. . . . . $_____
☐ MasterCard   ☐ VISA

Acct. No.   Exp. Date

Signature

Name   Telephone

Address

City/State/Zip

Call for FREE catalog

8/94   MasterCard and VISA Orders Accepted ($20 Minimum)

Muffins

This order blank may be photo-copied.